# Step-by-Step
# Cake Decorating

igloobooks

Published in 2013
by Igloo Books Ltd
Cottage Farm
Sywell
Northants
NN6 0BJ
www.igloobooks.com

Food photography and recipe development: PhotoCuisine UK
Front and back cover images © PhotoCuisine UK

OCE001 0813
2 4 6 8 10 9 7 5 3 1
ISBN: 978-1-78197-777-4

Printed and manufactured in China

# Step-by-Step
# Cake Decorating

# Contents

# Tools and Equipment

# Tools and Equipment

Whilst some cakes are very simple to decorate and require very little specialist equipment, there are others that will require you to have some more specialist tools to hand.

Icing Cutters: Cutters come in many different shapes and sizes, from simple circular cutters through to novelty shapes and push out cutters that also pattern the icing. They are available in most shops, but for more specialist equipment, you may have to look elsewhere. Try starting with some simple moulds, to help you practice your technique.

Cutters enable you to make much more precise shapes for decorating your cakes, and it's worth investing in a range of different sizes and shapes and building a collection up over time.

Cake Boards: Cake boards provide a stable hygienic base for your cakes and come in a variety of sizes and thicknesses. Generally you'll need cake boards that are about an inch / 2 cm wider than the base of your cake. If you are also decorating the boards with icing and novelties then you may need cake boards with a larger diameter.

Marble slab and chocolate tools: Making delicate chocolate decorations, such as curls, requires an ordered, clean and even work surface that remains cool such as a marble slab.

For chocolate work, have clean sharp tools at the ready. A new wallpaper scraper and pallet knives will enable you to more easily make chocolate curls and cigarillos. Greaseproof paper / baking parchment: These are used for lining cake tins, making piping bags and providing a non-stick surface to work sugarcraft on.

Sugarcraft tools: Specialist shops sell a wide range of tools designed specifically for decorating cakes. These include moulds for fondant, border cutters, crimpers, and modelling tools including:

- Bone tool: ideal for thinning and smoothing the edges of leaves, flower petals and frills.

- Serrated and tapered cone tool: used to indent into paste to create a cone shaped hollow, ideal for modelling marzipan fruits such as apples. The serrated cone is good for creating detailed and realistic throats of flowers.

- Scriber tool: is used for transcribing designs onto sugar plaques or cake sides, royal icing, sugarpaste or chocolate. The scriber tool is most useful to mark outlines of designs that you intend to pipe or paint onto a cake.

- Ball tool: a great tool to cup and shape leaves, petals and frills. The small end is ideal for creating detail on marzipan figures.

Foam modelling mats: these enable the cake decorator to easily and hygienically work with sugarpaste. The mat acts as a soft base to model delicate elements of sugarcraft, and also acts as a useful place to allow sugarcraft shapes to harden.

# Tools and Equipment

Heat lamps and latex gloves: When working with pulled sugar, you'll need to have a high powered heat lamp to keep the sugar malleable, and have a large box of latex gloves to provide hygienic protection from the heat of the sugar.

Cake polishers and rolling pins: In order to get a professional finish to your icing work, you'll need cake polishers to smooth out uneven blemishes in your fondant icing, and also to prepare flat even surfaces in your fondant icing. Rolling pins of different sizes will enable you to work with larger and smaller pieces of fondant, to create uniform thicknesses.

A clean set of paintbrushes are an essential tool for the cake decorator, and can be used for painting directly onto icing, sticking decorations to cakes, and manipulating and texturing sugarpaste. Always wash and dry your brushes thoroughly after use to prevent them from clogging.
Food coloring and paintbrushes: There are many different types and colors of food colorings using both natural and artificial ingredients. Liquid, gel and dry powder colorings are available and enable the cake decorator to color soft and hard fondants, cakes and sugar.

Cake tins: cake tins are another essential for the baker and cake decorator and its worth investing in a set of heavy bottomed cake tins of different sizes and shapes to enable you to create a wide variety of cakes.

Piping bags and nozzles: A sugarcraft staple, the cake decorator should have a good selection of piping bags and nozzles of various sizes to enable them to pipe different effects and different icings onto cakes.

Kitchen thermometer: For high heat sugar work, such as spinning sugar and pulling sugar, it's essential that you have a kitchen thermometer to measure the temperature of your mixtures to ensure that the techniques work properly.

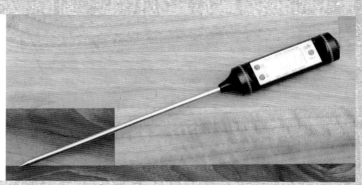

Pump action sugarpaste gun: Used to create a variety of fondant effects, where the consistency of the icing is too thick for standard piping. The guns come with a variety of apertures to create different shaped fondant ropes, hair, scallops and a huge range of fondant effects.

Measuring sets: Tape measures, rulers and rolling guides are other essential pieces of kit for the cake decorator. In order to accurately measure fondants, cakes, widths and depths the cake decorator should always have to hand set of accurate measuring tools.

Ribbons of all colors and sizes are great for tying around cakes, for an elegant finishing touch.

# Basic Recipes

# Basic Recipes
# Vanilla Sponge

## SERVES 16 | PREP TIME 15-20 minutes | COOKING TIME 40-45 minutes

## Ingredients

**For the sponge cake**

450 g / 1 lb / 3 cups self-raising
flour, sifted

450 g / 1 lb / 3 cups unsalted
butter, softened

450 g / 1 lb / 3 cups caster
(superfine) sugar

8 medium eggs, lightly beaten

2 tsp vanilla extract or seeds of 1 vanilla pod

a pinch of salt

## Method

1.  Preheat the oven to 170°C (150° fan) / 325F / gas 3.

2.  Grease and line two 8" square cake tins with greaseproof paper.

3.  Whisk the butter, sugar and vanilla in a bowl until pale and fluffy.

4.  Add the eggs, a little at a time, whilst whisking on low speed.

5.  Gently fold in the flour into the egg and butter mixture.

6.  Divide the batter evenly between the prepared cake tins.

7.  Bake for 35-40 minutes until golden and risen and a skewer comes out clean from their centres.

8.  Remove from the oven and let the sponges cool in their tins for 10 minutes before turning out onto a wire rack to cool completely; peel off any stuck greaseproof paper at this point.

9.  Wrap well and set aside for filling and decorating.

# Basic Recipes
# Chocolate Sponge

## SERVES 8 | PREP TIME 10-15 minutes | COOKING TIME 40-45 minutes

## Ingredients

**For the sponge cake**

225 g / 8 oz / 1 cup butter, softened

225 g / 8 oz / 1 cup caster sugar

4 medium eggs, lightly beaten

225 g / 8 oz / 1 ½ cups self raising
flour, sifted

4 tbs cocoa powder (sifted in with flour)

## Method

1. Preheat oven to 180°C (160° fan) / 425F / gas 4.

2. Line a tin with baking paper.

3. Whisk together butter and sugar until pale and fluffy.

4. Add the eggs slowly and combine, enusring that the mix does not curdle. If the mix should curdle add a small amount of the flour and continue.

5. Add flour and cocoa mix and slowly combine or fold in.

6. Spoon the mixture into the tin.

7. Place in oven for 30-35 minutes or until skewer comes out clean when inserted.

8. Turn out onto a wine rack to cool completely. Remove the baking paper from the sponge.

9. Wrap the cake and set aside for later use.

# Basic Recipes
# Round Fruit Cake

## SERVES 25 | PREP TIME 20-25 minutes | COOKING TIME 150 minutes

## Ingredients

175 g / 6 oz / 1 ⅙ cups plain flour

150 g / 5 oz / ¾ cup butter

150 g / 5 oz / ¾ cup soft brown sugar

2 large eggs

200 g / 7 oz / 1 cup currants

100 g / 3 ½ oz / ½ cup sultanas

100 g / 3 ½ oz / ½ cup raisins

65 g / 2 ½ oz / ⅓ cups glace cherries, quartered

50 g / 1 ¾ oz / ¼ cup mixed peel

50 g / 1 ¾ oz / ⅓ cup blanched chopped almonds

½ lemon, rind grated

½ tsp ground cinnamon

¼ tsp ground mixed spice

1 tsp black treacle

3 tbsp brandy

## Method

1. Pre-heat the oven to 150°C (130° fan) / 300F / gas 2.

2. Line a 6" round cake tin with two layers of baking parchment.

3. Combine currants, sultanas, raisins, glace cherries, mixed peel, almonds and lemon rind and mix.

4. Sift the flour and spices together into a bowl.

5. Cream the butter and sugar, in another bowl until it is light and fluffy.

6. Add the eggs one at a time following each one with one spoon of flour.

7. Fold in the remaining ingredients until mixed. Add the black treacle, too.

8. Spoon the mixture into the tin and make a slight hollow in the centre of the mixture to ensure the cake stays flat during baking.

9. Tie two layers of brown paper around the outside of the tin, then bake for two and a half hours.

10. Remove from the oven and allow to cool in the tin.

11. Turn the cake onto a wire rack and prick the cake all over with a metal skewer.

12. Spoon over the brandy and wrap well and store until needed.

# Basic Recipes

# Cupcakes

## SERVES 20-25 | PREP TIME 10-15 minutes | COOKING TIME 15-20 minutes

## Ingredients

### For the cupcakes

225 g / 8 oz / 1 ½ cups self raising flour

225 g / 8 oz / 1 cup caster sugar

225 g / 8 oz / 1 cup butter softened

4 medium eggs, beaten

½ vanilla pod, seeds only

### For the buttercream

250 g / 9 oz / 1 ⅙ cups butter

350 g / 12 oz / 3 cups icing sugar, sieved

pinch of salt

food coloring

vanilla seeds

## Method

1. Preheat the oven to 190ºC (170º fan) / 375F / gas 5.

2. Line a muffin tray with cupcake cases.

3. In a mixing bowl beat together the butter and sugar until pale and fluffy.

4. Slowly add the eggs a little at a time whilst beating the mixture on medium speed.

5. Add the flour and combine on a low speed, or fold in using a large spoon.

6. Pipe the mix into the cake cases until they are two thirds full, making sure not to get any mix on the side of the cases.

7. Place the trays in the oven and bake for 12-15 minutes or until firm to the touch.

8. Cool the cakes slightly in the tin and place on a wire rack to cool completely.

9. To make the buttercream, beat the butter, salt and vanilla in a bowl.

10. Add the icing sugar a spoon at a time, beating to incorporate between each spoonful.

11. Once all the icing sugar has been added, incorporate the food coloring and beat the mix on high speed for 3-4 minutes until light and fluffy.

12. Using a large star shaped nozzle, pipe swirls, starting from the outside of the cake, into the centre.

# Basic Recipes
# Classic Victoria Sponge

## SERVES 8 | PREP TIME 10-15 minutes | COOKING TIME 20-30 minutes

## Ingredients

225 g / 8 oz / 1 cup caster sugar

225 g / 8 oz / 1 cup butter, softened

4 eggs beaten

225 g / 8 oz / 1 ½ cups self raising flour

1 tsp baking powder

2 tbsp milk

**To fill…**

150 g / 5 oz / ¾ cup strawberry jam

300 ml / 10 ½ fl. oz / 1 ¼ cups fresh whipping cream

**or**

300ml / 10 ½ fl. oz / 1 ¼ cups buttercream

## Method

1.  Preheat the oven to 190° C (170° fan) / 375F/ gas 5.

2.  Line two 8" inch tins with baking paper.

3.  Beat all ingredients together in a bowl until smooth.

4.  Divide the mix between the tins and smooth with the back of a spoon.

5.  Place in oven for 20 minutes or until golden and the cake springs back when pressed lightly.

6.  Remove from oven and allow to cool in the tin.

7.  Turn the cakes onto a wire rack and fill with butter cream and jam.

8.  Dust with icing sugar and serve.

# Basic Recipes
# Basic Chocolate Log

## SERVES 8 | PREP TIME 15-20 minutes | COOKING TIME 30-35 minutes

## Ingredients

### For the sponge cake

250 g / 9 oz / 1 ¼ cups unsalted butter, softened

250 g / 9 oz / 1 ¼ cups caster (superfine) sugar

4 medium eggs, lightly beaten

250 g / 9 oz / 1 ¼ cups self raising flour, sifted

4 tbs cocoa (sifted in with flour)

### For the chocolate buttercream

125 g / 4 ½ oz / ½ cup unsalted butter, softened

175 g / 6 oz / 1 ½ cups icing sugar, sifted

100 g / 3 ½ oz / ⅔ cup dark chocolate, melted

## Method

1. Preheat oven to 180°C (160° fan) / 350F / gas 4.

2. Grease and line a swiss-roll tin with baking paper.

3. Whisk together butter and sugar until pale and fluffy.

4. Add the eggs slowly and combine.

5. Add flour/cocoa mix and slowly combine or fold in.

6. Divide mixture between 2 tins and place in oven for 30-35 minutes or until skewer comes out clean when inserted.

7. Allow the cake to slightly cool in the tin

8. Whilst the cake is cooling, dampen a tea towel and place on a chopping board.

9. Carefully turn out the sponge onto the board with the towel.

10. Trim the sponge if necessary and then score along the short edge, about 1 cm deep to help with starting the roll.

11. Once the sponge has cooled further, spread with butter cream filling.

12. Starting with the scored edge, carefully roll the sponge to form a log shape.

# Basic Recipes
# Chocolate Collar Cake

## SERVES 1 | PREP TIME 10-15 minutes plus cooking time for cake

## Ingredients

Round sponge cake or chocolate sponge
125 g / 4 ½ oz / ¾ cup milk or dark
chocolate
30 g / 1 oz / ⅕ cup white chocolate
400 g / 14 oz / 1 ¾ cups chocolate
buttercream

1 strip greaseproof paper, acetate or
cellophane sheet, cut slightly wider than the
height of the cake and long enough to circle
the cake

## Method

1. Melt the different chocolates gently over separate Bain-Maries, making sure that the water doesn't touch the bottom of the bowls.

2. Cover the cake with chocolate buttercream, ensuring an even application.

3. When melted, drizzle the white chocolate in a random pattern across the strip of greaseproof paper and allow to cool and harden.

4. Spread the milk or dark chocolate over the strip of greaseproof paper, acetate or cellophane with a pallet knife.

5. Place the collar, milk or dark chocolate side down, around the cake, carefully adhering it to the buttercream, seal with a little tape and place in the refrigerator to set.

6. When chocolate has hardened, carefully remove the greaseproof paper.

7. Trim the collar down with a heated sharp knife so that it provides a small lip.

8. Decorate with chocolate flakes.

# Basic Recipes
# Basic Macaroons

## SERVES 15 | PREP TIME 20-25 minutes | COOKING TIME 10-15 minutes

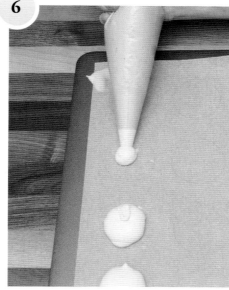

## Ingredients

175 g / 6 oz / 1 ½ cups icing sugar

125 g / 4 ½ oz / 1 cup ground almonds

3 large egg whites, at room temperature

75 g / 3 oz / ⅓ cup caster (superfine) sugar

food coloring

your filling of choice

## Method

1. Preheat the oven to 140°C (120° fan) / 275F / gas 1. On a sheet of baking parchment, use a pencil to draw 30 even-sized circles. Then turn the paper over and place on a baking sheet.

2. Place the icing sugar and ground almonds in a food processor and pulse, then pass through a sieve, discarding anything left in the sieve.

3. In a clean bowl, whisk the egg whites until they form soft peaks. Add the caster sugar and whisk until thick and glossy and stiff peaks are formed.

4. Add any colors or flavourings. Fold in half the almond mix, using a spatula.

5. Add the remaining almonds and continue folding until everything is fully mixed together.

6. Transfer the mixture to a piping bag with a 1cm diameter round nozzle and pipe onto the baking sheets using the circles as a guide.

7. Tap the baking sheets firmly onto a work surface to expel any air bubbles. Leave to stand to 10-15 minutes.

8. Bake in the oven for 10-15 minutes. Remove and allow to cool completely before removing from the baking sheet.

9. Sandwich your choice of filling between two macaroons. Repeat to make 15 finished macaroons.

# Basic Recipes
# Chocolate Ganache

## SERVES 6 | PREP TIME 10-15 minutes

## Ingredients

225 g / 8 oz / 1 ½ cups dark chocolate
(maximum 55% cocoa solids)

175 ml / 6 fl oz / ¾ cup double cream

## Method

1. In a heatproof bowl, break the chocolate into small pieces.

2. In a pan, bring the cream to a rolling boil and then remove from the heat.

3. Pour the cream straight onto the chocolate pieces

4. Stir the mix vigorously to combine

5. Set the mixture aside to cool or use straight away if covering a cake.

6. If the ganache has been chilled, bring it up to room temperature and whisk before using.

# Basic Recipes
# Royal Icing

SERVES Cover 8" round cake | PREP TIME 10-15 minutes

Traditionally the mainstay of the wedding cake, Royal icing is an important element of the cake decorators materials. It allows intricate details to be applied onto wedding and celebration cakes and other treats and is perfect for piping swags, lettering, scallops and a host of other decorative techniques.

Royal icing is easy to make and versatile and dried to a hard finish. It can also be colored easily with gel food coloring to match the decorator's color scheme. Piping Royal icing takes practice. Once you have the Royal icing to the right consistency, it's advisable to practice on a sheet of greaseproof paper before applying the icing onto the cake.

## Ingredients

675 g / 1 lb 8 oz / 6 cups icing sugar
3 egg whites
2-3 teaspoons of strained lemon juice

## Method

1. Sift the icing sugar.

2. In a clean bowl whisk the egg whites until just frothy.

3. Add half the icing sugar and beat together using a wooden spoon.

4. Add the lemon juice and half the remaining icing sugar and then continue beating until the icing becomes smooth and white.

5. Add the rest of the icing sugar a little at a time until soft peaks are formed.

6. This can now be divided and colored as required.

7. Place the icing in an airtight container until needed.

# Techniques

Techniques
# Piping Work

Piping icing can be a daunting task for anyone new to cake decorating. It's a skill that takes a lot of practice to get right. Once mastered, it will allow the cake decorator to perform a wide range of creative tasks including scalloping, swags, ropes, flowers, leaves and many other effects.

Make the royal icing as per the recipe on the previous page, and ensure that its kept in an airtight container to prevent it from hardening and drying out. The royal icing needs to be stiff enough to hold its form yet malleable enough to be piped through a small piping nozzle.

## How to make a piping bag and pipe royal icing:

1. Take a large square of greaseproof paper and fold diagonally in half.

2. Use a pallet knife or scissors to cut down the fold.

3. Hold the longest side edge of the triangle in one hand and one tip of the triangle in the other hand.

4. Curl the bottom corner under itself and in toward the upper corner to create a cone shape.

5. Roll the cone toward the other end of the triangle until all of the paper is wrapped around the cone and fold the top to secure.

6. Fold the rim of the open end in on itself. This will secure the cone shape.

7. Cut the point off the cone to accommodate the size of the piping nozzle you are using. Insert the piping nozzle and secure in place with a piping bag collar.

8. Fill the bag with royal icing.

9. Press the open end together and fold over to keep the icing from spilling out.

10. Take a sheet of greaseproof paper and practice your piping patterns before you attempt to pipe directly onto a cake.

11. Practice swirls, swags and dotting and experiment with different piping nozzles to get practiced in creating the effects you can achieve using this method of cake decorating.

12. Once you feel confident enough, pipe the patterns you want to create onto your cake.

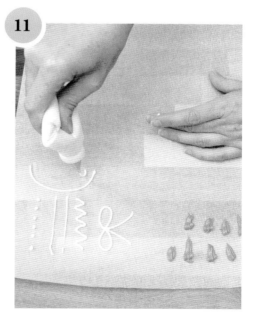

Techniques

# Fondant Icing Work

Fondant icing underpins many different cake decorating techniques, and is a durable, malleable and extremely versatile material. It can be used to ice cakes, make novelty figures, flowers, plaques and decorations.

Fondant can be purchased at most supermarkets and all good cake decorating shops. Like marzipan its worth buying good quality fondant as it will keep for longer.

Fondant icing can be easily colored using food colorings, and will harden when left open to the air to make a smooth surface ideal for decorating and painting.

## How to use fondant icing:

1. Knead the block of fondant on a silicon mat until its soft and malleable, this will make it easier to roll and use for modelling.

2. Use gel food coloring to color the icing. Add a little at a time and knead it into the fondant until you reach the desired color. Knead the color into the fondant until the icing is a uniform color.

3. To cover a cake, measure the sides and diameter / width and ensure that you have enough fondant rolled out to cover the top and sides of the cake.

4. When rolled out, use a rolling pin to drape the fondant sheet over the cake.

5. Smooth over the cake using your hands.

6. Use cake buffers dusted with a little icing sugar to obtain a smooth professional finish.

7. Trim any excess with a sharp knife.

8. Rolled fondant can be used to make cut out shapes and plaques, and can also be used to cover cake boards.

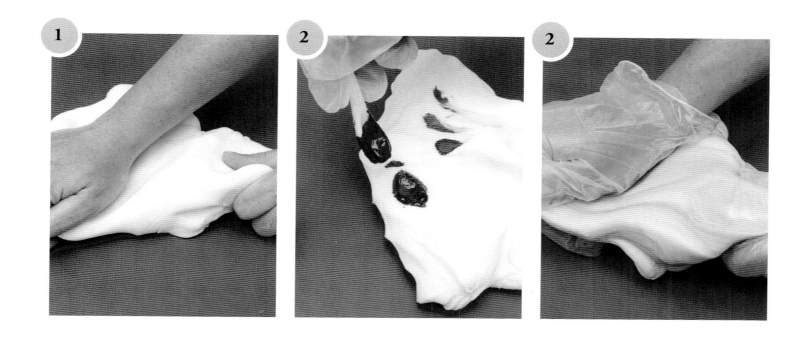

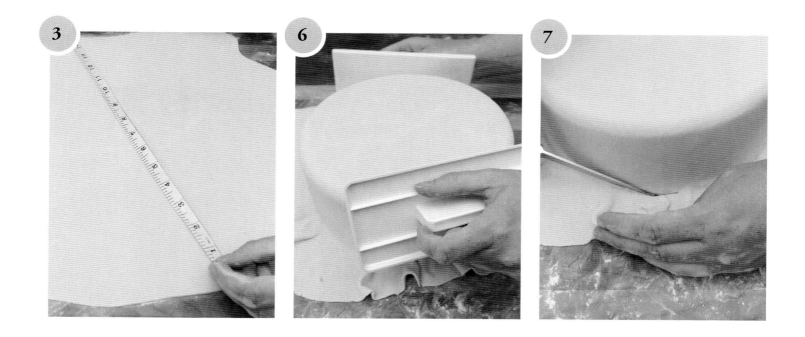

Techniques

# Marzipan Work

Marzipan work is a core component of cake decorating. It's used to line fruitcakes, sponge cakes and provide a smooth surface on which to place fondant icing. It can also be used in its own right as a form of icing.

Marzipan is widely available and can be purchased from most supermarkets and also cake decorating shops. It's worth buying good quality marzipan as it will remain malleable and keep for longer.

## How to ice cakes using marzipan:

1. Its important to knead your marzipan when you begin to work with it. This will make it softer and easier to work with.

2. Once kneaded use a rolling pin dusted with icing sugar to get the marzipan to the desired thickness for whatever you are using it for.

3. Small balls of marzipan can be used to press into and plug holes in fruit cake to make an even surface for icing.

4. Marzipan should be adhered to cakes using a sieved jam, this will ensure a good bond between the icing layers and the cake.

5. Once rolled to the correct thickness, drape the marzipan over a large rolling pin and place the marzipan sheet over the cake.

6. Using your hands, smooth the marzipan onto the corners and sides of the cake, ensuring that its completely.

7. Trim away any excess marzipan and wrap in cling film to keep for another cake.

8. Use cake buffers dusted with a little icing sugar buff the marzipan to obtain a smooth professional finish.

9. To make marzipan shapes, use cutters and sugarpaste tools to create shapes and textures. Marzipan can also be used to model figures and novelties.

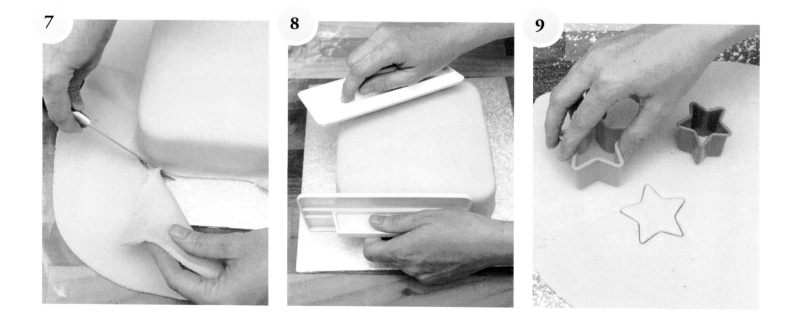

# Delicious Cakes

33

# Chocolate Rose Cake

## Ingredients

Chocolate sponge cake (see page 15)

400 g / 14 oz / 2 cups dark chocolate fondant icing (see pages 28-29)

110 g / 4 oz dark chocolate, melted

## SERVES 8 | PREP TIME 1 hour

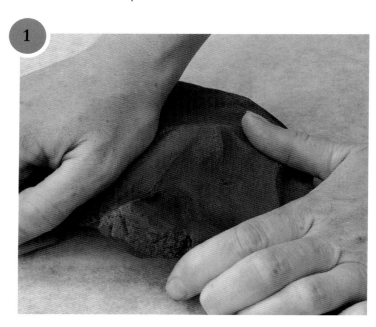

Knead the chocolate fondant icing until pliable.

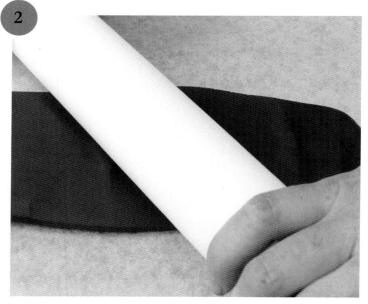

Roll out the fondant onto a piece of greaseproof paper. Spread the centre of the top of the cake with melted chocolate.

**3**

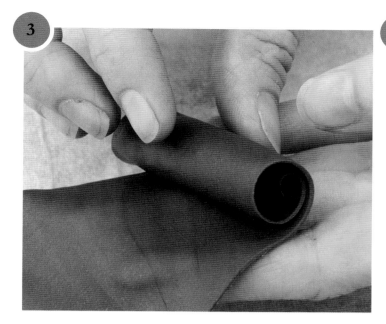

Cut the chocolate fondant sheet into thick strips. Start rolling the edge of the first strip into a tight curl.

**4**

Transfer it to the top of the cake and continue to wrap the fondant ribbon loosely around.

**5**

Build up the layers with more strips until the whole of the top of the cake is covered.

# Coconut Cake

## Ingredients

### For the sponge cake

400 g / 1 lb / 2 cups caster (superfine) sugar

400 g / 1 lb / 4 cups self raising flour

400 g / 1 lb / 2 cups butter, softened

8 medium eggs

80 g / 3 oz / 1 cup desiccated coconut

½ lemon, zested

### Coconut buttercream

250 g / 9 oz / 1 cup butter, softened

175 g / 6 oz / 1 ¼ cups icing sugar, sieved

40 g / 1 ½ oz / ½ cup desiccated coconut

## SERVES 8 | PREP TIME 30 minutes

Line a 20 cm / 8" cake tin and follow the method for making a basic sponge (see page 14) but add the coconut to the mixture.

Mix the icing sugar, butter and coconut together to make a smooth buttercream.

When cooled, slice the cake in half and place the top half to one side.

When cooled, sandwich the two cakes with the coconut buttercream.

Lay the top of the cake carefully on top. Coat the entire cake with buttercream and sprinkle with coconut.

# Fraisier

## Ingredients

Round vanilla sponge cake
(see page 14)
400 g / 1 lb / 2 cups strawberries,
hulled and halved
400 ml / 13 fl. oz / 1 ½ cups double cream
100 g / 3 ½ oz / 1 cup icing sugar
2 leaves of gelatine

## SERVES 6 | PREP TIME 1 hour 30 minutes

Take a sponge and trim around the edge of the cake to remove the rust.

Slice the cake horizontally to make 2 thin discs of sponge cake.
Place one slice into a round baking tin.

Whip the cream and icing sugar together until the mixture becomes stiff.

Line the bottom slice of cake with strawberry halves and around the inside of the tin.

Fill the tin with the whipped cream and smooth the top. Place in the refrigerator to allow the cream to firm.

Whilst chilling, soak the gelatine in some cold water. Blend the strawberries and pass them through a sieve to extract the juice and remove the seeds. Gently heat in a pan.

Remove the gelatine from the water and add to the strawberry juice and stir until dissolved. Remove from the heat and pour into a bowl.

Remove from the chilling bowl and mix in 1 tbsp of double cream.

Take the sponge from the refrigerator and place the last sponge slice on top.

When the strawberry jelly is almost set, pour over the last sponge tier. Chill to set and then carefully remove the tin and decorate with leftover cream and strawberries.

# Cherry Chocolate Fan Cake

## Ingredients

Chocolate sponge cake
(see page 15)

400 g / 14 oz dark chocolate, chopped

350 ml / 12 fl. oz / 1 ½ cups double cream

110 g / 4 oz / ½ cup apricot jam

200 g / 7 oz / 1 cup dark chocolate fondant icing (see pages 28-29)

6 fresh cherries, stoned

icing sugar to dust

edible gold leaf

## SERVES 8 | PREP TIME 2 hours

Melt the chocolate in a bain-marie and leave to cool a little.

Stir in the cream and mix well.

Melt the jam in the microwave then brush over the top and sides of the cake.

Pour the chocolate ganache on top of the cake and use a palette knife to smooth it down the sides.

Knead the chocolate fondant icing until pliable and roll out on a non-stick mat.

Cut the icing into strips and cut the edges at an angle.

Ripple the icing with your fingers, then spread one side out to create a fan.

Pinch the bottom of the fan to secure.

Arrange half of the fans around the edge of the cake. Arrange the rest of the fans in a ring on top of the cake.

Dust the fan ring lightly with icing sugar. Spoon the cherries into the centre and finish with some gold leaf.

# Chocolate Curl Cake

## Ingredients

110 g / 4 oz / ½ cup apricot jam

round chocolate sponge cake (see page 15)

400 g / 14 oz dark chocolate, melted

## SERVES 8 | PREP TIME 1 hour

Melt the jam in the microwave then brush over the top and sides of the cake.

Pour ¾ of the melted chocolate on top of the cake.

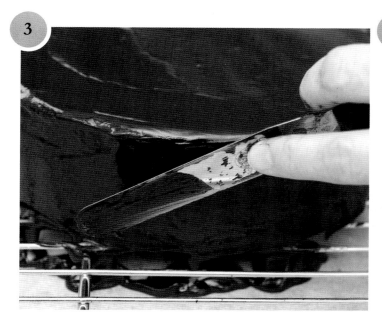

Use a palette knife to smooth the top and spread it evenly down the sides and leave to chill.

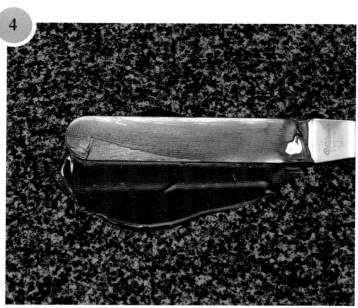

Spread the rest of the chocolate in a thin layer onto a marble slab. Leave to set.

Use a meat cleaver at a 45° degree angle to make chocolate curls.

Carefully place the curls onto the cake.

# Chocolate Biscuit Cake

## Ingredients

6 round biscuits

400 g / 14 oz / 1 ¾ cups chocolate ganache (see page 22)

225 g / 8 oz dark chocolate, melted

150 g / 5 oz / 1 cup raspberries

## SERVES 6 | PREP TIME 1 hour

Spread a third of the chocolate onto a sheet of cellophane and spread out into an 8 cm / 3" circle. Leave to set.

Coat the biscuit bases with the rest of the chocolate.

Pipe the ganache in a spiral around the chocolate biscuit.

Reserve 1 raspberry for decoration and pile the rest in the centre of the cake. Top with a second chocolate biscuit and pipe the rest of the ganache to encase the raspberries in a big swirl.

Peel the chocolate medallion off of the cellophane and set it on top of the ganache.

Top with the reserved raspberry for decoration.

# Basket Weave Cake

## Ingredients

fruit cake (see page 16)

500 g / 17 oz / 2 cups white fondant icing (see pages 28-29)

400 g / 14 oz / 1 ½ cups royal icing (see page 23 and 26-27)

200 g / 7 oz / 1 cup buttercream

selection of fresh seasonal flowers

## SERVES 4 | PREP TIME 1 hour 30 minutes

Cover a cake board using the fondant icing.

Using a palette knife, coat the sponge in buttercream and place in the refrigerator to set.

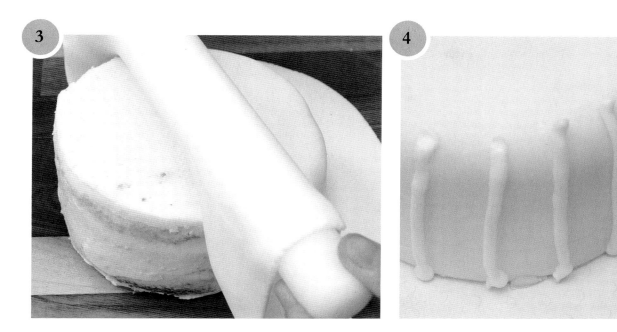

Cover the cake in fondant icing and allow to dry.

Using a number 2 plain nozzle, pipe vertical straight lines in royal icing.

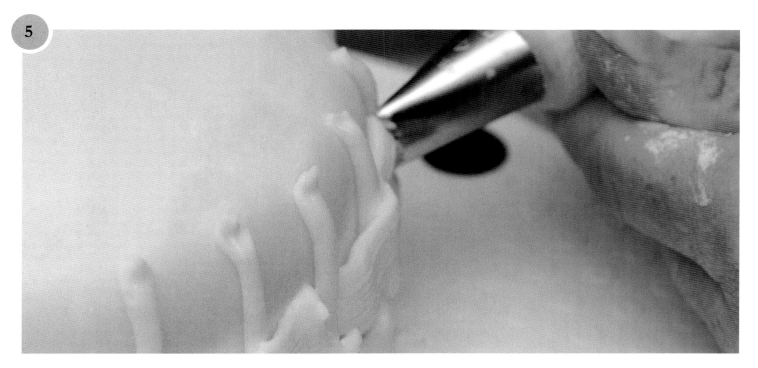

Pipe horizontal lines, using a basket weave nozzle, over 1 vertical line and then stop at the next vertical line and begin again at the other side of that line.

**6**

Using the same nozzle, pipe scallops around the top and the bottom of the cake and allow to set.

**7**

Decorate with fresh flowers.

# Hand Painted Cake

## Ingredients

Sponge vanilla cake (see page 14)

500 g / 1 lb 3 oz / 2 cups white fondant

edible food dusts, various colours

rejuvenator spirit

ribbon, to decorate

### Equipment

scriber needle

paintbrushes

icing pen

## SERVES 6 | PREP TIME 1 hour 30 minutes

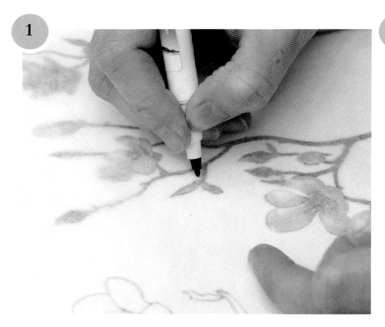

Draw a design on parchment using an edible icing pen.

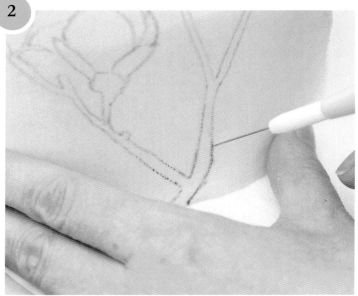

Carefully lay the design on the cake and, using a scribing tool, prick the cake along the lines of the design.

**3**

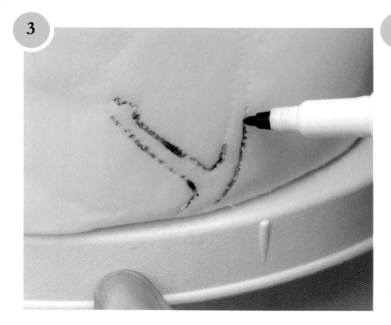

Remove the parchment and, using the icing pen, draw a faint outline along the marks in the fondant.

**4**

Take the different coloured dusts and mix with rejuvenator spirit.

**5**

Use a thin brush to paint the outline of the petals.

**6**

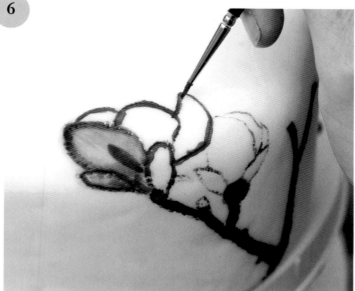

Carefully fill in the lines using more dust and rejuvenator spirit.

**7**

Repeat step 5 and 6 for the leaves and the branches. Leave to dry for 2 hours.

**8**

Choose a complementary ribbon to fix along the bottom of the cake and secure using double sided adhesive tape.

# Chocolate Bay Leaf Cake

## Ingredients

110 g / 4 oz / 1 cup dark chocolate, chopped

7 fresh bay leaves

200 g / 7 oz / 1 cup granulated sugar

8 hazelnuts

round chocolate sponge cake (see page 15)

2 tbsp icing sugar

## SERVES 8 | PREP TIME 1 hour 30 minutes

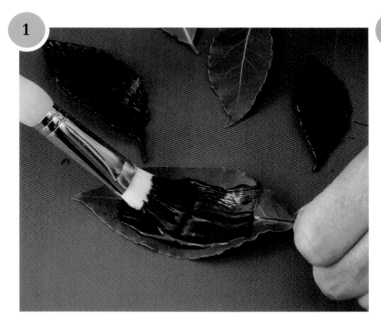

Melt the chocolate in a microwave or bain-marie. Paint the melted chocolate onto the back of the bay leaves and leave to set.

Carefully peel away the leaves from the chocolate.

Stick a cocktail stick into each hazelnut to help coat them in the caramel.

Put the sugar in a heavy bottomed saucepan and heat until it starts to melt around the edges. Gently swirl the pan over the heat until it has all melted.

Dip the hazelnuts into the caramel and leave them to drip upside down over the pan until the caramel has hardened.

Dust the cake with icing sugar. Assemble the leaves and caramel coated hazelnuts on top of the cake.

# Iced Butterfly Cake

## Ingredients

Filled Victoria sponge cake (see page 18)

100 g / 4 oz / ½ cups royal icing (see page 23)

400 g / 13 oz / 2 cups purple fondant icing (see pages 28-29)

purple edible glitter gel

edible copper shimmer dust

edible icing pen

## SERVES 8 | PREP TIME 2 hours

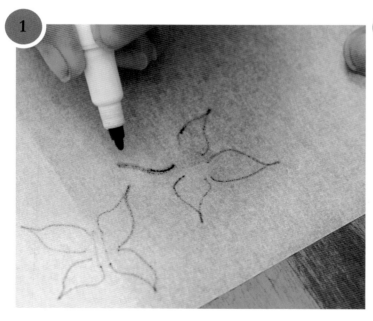

Cover a four inch sponge in purple fondant and allow it to harden. Using an icing pen, draw a butterfly design on a piece of baking parchment.

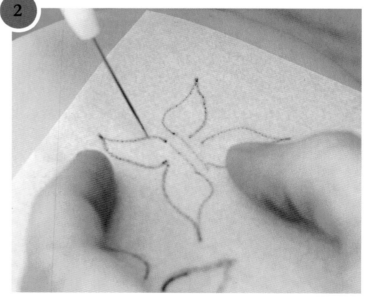

Gently place the parchment onto the cake and using a scribing needle, mark a series of small holes along the pattern.

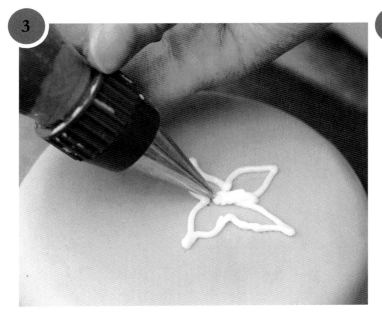

Remove the parchment and pipe royal icing along the dotted lines and allow to set.

Using a soft small brush, gently apply the shimmer dust inside the piped butterflies.

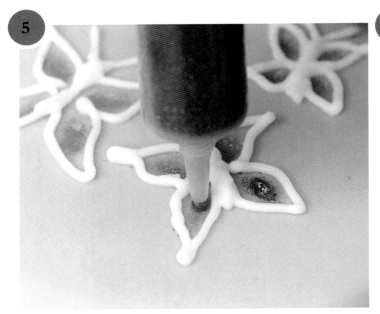

Then carefully pipe on the glitter gel.

Using a scriber needle pull the gel out to the corners to match the butterfly design. To finish the cake, secure a ribbon around the base of the cake using adhesive tape.

# Coffee Macaroon Cake

## Ingredients

12 small chocolate filled macaroons
(see page 21)
4 sheets gelatine
2 tsp coffee essence
200 g / 7 oz / 1 cup caster sugar
600 ml / 30 fl. oz / 3 cups double cream
small handful chocolate covered coffee beans
1 pack of gold sugared almonds
2 tsp silver dragees
ribbon to decorate

## SERVES 6-8 | PREP TIME 45 minutes

Soften the gelatine in cold water. Pour the cream, coffee essence and sugar into a saucepan and bring to the boil. Remove from the heat. Dissolve the gelatine into the cream mixture, stirring constantly until dissolved.

Divide the preparation into two moulds, one wider than the other by at least the width of the macaroons.

**3**

Cool for 4 hours until it has set. Stand the moulds in a bowl of warm water for a moment or two, then carefully slide a pallet knife around the edges of the moulds.

**4**

Turn the larger mould out onto a serving plate and then turn out the second mould onto the middle of the top of the first mould.

**5**

Take one macaroon and push the dragees around the rim of just one.

**6**

Arrange the remaining macaroons around the circumference of the bottom layer.

Stand the sugared almonds against the sides of the top layer of the dessert.

Arrange the coffee beans around the top layer of the dessert.

Top off with the dragee macaroon. Tie a ribbon around the base layer and serve.

# Chestnut Flan

## Ingredients

100 g / 3 ½ oz / ½ cup butter, softened

500 g / 17 oz / 2 cups chestnut pureé

pinch of nutmeg

pinch of salt

4 eggs

2 egg yolks

500 g / 17 oz / 2 ¼ cups shortcrust pastry

5 sheets of filo pastry

8 candied chestnuts

1 vanilla pod

gold leaf

orange zest

icing sugar, for dusting

## SERVES 6 | PREP TIME 15 minutes | COOKING TIME 1 hour

Preheat the oven to 180ºC (160° fan) / 350F, gas 4. Prepare and measure all of the ingredients.

Line a greased flan tin with shortcrust pastry and fill with baking beans. Blind bake for 15 minutes. Remove from the oven, discard the beans and return to the oven for 5 minutes.

61

**3**

In a bowl, mix together the butter, chestnut pureé, nutmeg and salt.

**4**

In a separate bowl whisk together the eggs and egg yolks and combine with the chestnut mix.

**5**

Pour the mix into the pastry case and place in the oven for 35 minutes until the mixture has cooked.

**6**

Cut the filo pastry into equal sized squares and brush with melted butter.

**7**

Lay one sheet on top of another sheet at oblique angles to make a star shape. Scrunch the sheets in the centre to form a flower shape and place in a muffin tin to retain their shape whilst baking.

**8**

Place in the oven and remove when crisp and golden. When the flan is cool, dust with icing sugar.

**9**

Arrange the filo flowers on top. Scatter the candied chestnuts and orange zest around the flowers.

**10**

Arrange the vanilla pod so that it stands up. Gild the candied chestnuts with the edible gold leaf.

# Sugar-spun Heart Cake

## Ingredients

Vanilla sponge cake, heart-shaped
(see page 14)
100 g / 3 ½ oz / ½ cup caster (superfine) sugar
40 ml / 1 ½ fl oz / ½ cup water
pink food dye

## SERVES 4 | PREP TIME 45 minutes

Prepare and measure all of the ingredients.

Place the sugar and water in a heavy bottomed saucepan and heat gently.

Slowly bring the syrup to a boil and when it begins to change colour remove the pan from the heat. Set the pan aside and allow to cool for 5 minutes.

Add a few drops of the pink food dye and stir.

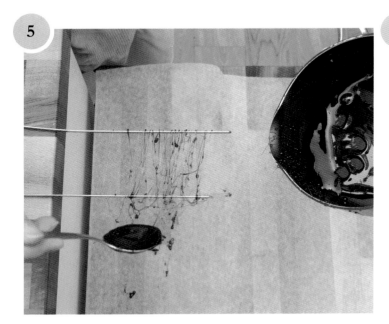

Using a spoon, drizzle the syrup over 2 metal skewers in a backward and forward motion.

When enough strands have formed, carefully remove from the skewers and place carefully over the cake.

# Apple Bavarian

## Ingredients

**For the Bavarian**

3 apples, peeled, cored and quartered

½ lemon

30 g / 1 oz / butter

100 g / 3 ½ oz / sugar

4 egg yolks whipped

60 g / 2 oz / ¼ cup honey

200 ml / 6 ½ fl oz / ¾ cup milk

100 g / 3 ½ oz / ¾ cup maple syrup

4 sheets of gelatine

300 ml / 10 fl. oz / 1 ¼ cups double cream

**For the decoration**

250 g / 9 oz / 1 ¼ cup sugar

3 tbsp water

walnut halves

## SERVES 4-6 | PREP TIME 1 hour 15 minutes

Cover the apple segments in lemon juice to stop them going brown. Melt the butter and sugar in a wide frying pan. Sautee the apples until golden brown. Remove from the heat and allow to cool.

Mix the whipped egg yolks with the milk, honey and maple syrup and heat gently in a saucepan. Meanwhile, soften the gelatine in cold water, and wring it out.

Add the gelatine to the egg, milk and honey mixture and stir continuously until it dissolves. Pour into a bowl which is sitting inside a larger bowl of iced water. Whip in the cream and combine. Allow to cool.

Line a 6-8 inch loose bottom tin with film. Place the apple segments around the sides and base of the tin. Pour in the cream mixture and place in the refrigerator for 3 hours to set.

In a pan, mix the sugar and water together and heat over a high heat until it begins to caramelize. Using a fork, very carefully dip the walnut halves into the syrup and place on a greaseproof sheet to cool.

Using a fork drizzle the remaining syrup across a sheet of greaseproof paper into a random pattern. Allow to cool completely. Decorate the Bavarian with the caramelized walnuts and sugar crackling.

# Pistachio and Cherry Cake

## Ingredients

3 eggs

100 g / 3 ½ oz / 1 cup plain flour

80 g / 3oz / ¾ cup shelled, unsalted pistachios

3 ½ g / 1 tsp baking powder

100 g / 3 ½ oz / ½ cup butter

pinch of salt

green food colouring

angelica to decorate

**Buttercream**

100 g / 3 ½ oz butter

160 g / 5 oz icing sugar, sifted

green food colouring

60 g / 2 oz shelled, unsalted pistachios

## SERVES 4-6 | PREP TIME 1 hour 15 minutes

Place the pistachios in a food processor and pulse until they form a fine powder.

In a mixing bowl, beat the eggs and sugar for 5 minutes until thick and creamy.

68

**3**

Sift the flour, baking powder and salt into another bowl. Add one third of the flour mix to the egg mixture and fold. Then gently fold in 80 g / 3 oz / ¾ cup of the powdered pistachios.

**4**

Melt the butter in a saucepan and remove any scum that forms on the surface. Add the melted clarified butter and fold in with remaining third of flour and 2 drops of green food colouring.

**5**

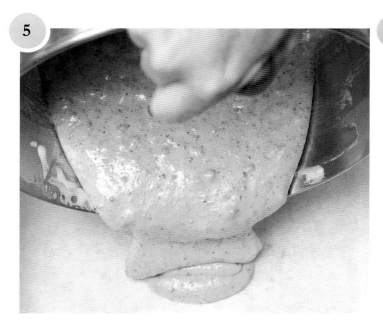

Spoon the mix into a lined square tin and bake for 25-35 minutes at 180ºC (160ºC fan) / 425F / gas4 until it shrinks away from the tin or if a skewer comes out clean once inserted.

**6**

For the buttercream, beat the butter and the icing sugar in a mixing bowl until it becomes light and fluffy.

**7**

Add the green food colouring a little at a time to reach the desired shade.
Fold in the remaining powdered pistachios.

**8**

Slice and layer the cake with buttercream.

**9**

Dust the top of the cake with large grains of sugar.

**10**

Decorate the cake with green glace cherries and strips of angelica.

# White Chocolate and Cherry Cake

## Ingredients

Chocolate sponge cake (see page 15)

300 g / 10 ½ oz / 2 cups white chocolate, broken into pieces

175 ml / 6 fl. oz / ¾ cup double cream

1 tin of cherries

few cherries for decoration

30 g / 1 oz / ¼ cup good quality dark chocolate

cherry syrup

rose leaves

## SERVES 4-6 | PREP TIME 1 hour

Heat the syrup from the tin of cherries in a pan and boil until the syrup reduces by half.

Bring the double cream to a rolling boil and then pour onto 225g of the chocolate. Stir the chocolate until it has all melted and formed a glossy ganache (see page 22).

**3**

Melt the dark chocolate slowly in a bowl over a pan of simmering water. Wash and thoroughly dry the cherries and then partially dip them in chocolate. Set them aside on baking parchment to set.

**4**

Using a small brush paint the chocolate onto the smooth surface of the rose leaf and place on the parchment to set.

**5**

Slice the cakes and brush with the reduced syrup. Scatter the tinned cherries onto the sponge.

**6**

Smooth over the ganache and place the remaining cake slice on top.

Melt the remaining white chocolate and pour some onto a marble slab, retaining some to cover the cake. Using a palette knife smooth the chocolate over the marble until it sets. Create curls by pushing a flat bladed knife over the surface of the white chocolate.

Cover the cake in the ganache and then pour a small amount of white chocolate onto the top of the cake.

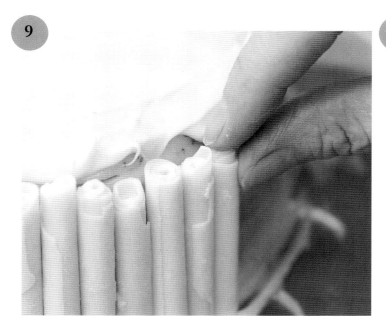

Stick the curls onto the side of the cake. Add the chocolate-dipped cherries on top.

Carefully remove the leaves from the chocolate and place them on to the cake. Tie a ribbon around the outside of the cake.

# Chocolate, Pear and Chestnut Gateau

## Ingredients

3 pears, peeled

1 cinnamon stick

55 g / 2 oz / ¼ cup butter

55 g / 2 oz / ¼ cup demerara sugar

round chocolate sponge cake

(see page 15)

400 g / 14 oz / 1 ¾ cups sweetened chestnut puree

110 g / 4 oz dark chocolate, melted

marrons glace

## SERVES 8 | PREP TIME 1 hour 30 minutes

Cover the pears and cinnamon with water and poach for 10 minutes or until soft. Drain the pears, then cut 2 of them in half and remove the cores.

Return the pear halves to the pan with the butter and sugar and cook over a low heat until the sugar has dissolved and the pears are lightly caramelised.

**3**

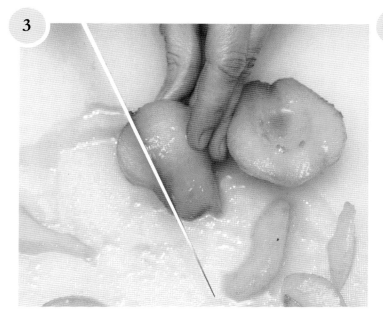

Leave the pears to cool and then slice them.

**4**

Divide the cake and fill with chestnut puree, then cover the top and sides.

**5**

Fan the pear slices around the outside of the cake and then pour on the melted chocolate. Spread out using a palette knife.

**6**

Arrange the marrons glace and the reserved poached pear on top of the cake. Dust the cake with icing sugar.

# Ice Cream Macaroon Cake

## Ingredients

20 different flavoured macaroons (see page 21)

20 scoops of ice cream

250 ml / 8.5 fl. oz / 1 cup double cream

3 egg whites

150 g / 5 oz / 1 ¼ cup caster (super fine) sugar

½ tsp cornflour

½ tsp white wine vinegar

redcurrants

raspberries

## SERVES 6 | PREP TIME 30 minutes

Line a baking sheet with baking paper. Draw 1 large circle and 1 medium circle on the paper and then turn the paper over. Whisk the egg whites and half the sugar until soft peaks are formed.

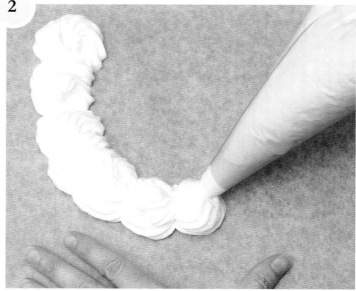

Add the remaining sugar and whisk until firm peaks are formed. Fold in the cornflour and vinegar and spoon the mix into a piping bag. Pipe the meringue onto the baking paper using the circles as a guide.

**3**

Bake in the oven for 10 minutes at 140ºC (120 ° fan) / 240F / gas 2. Then turn the oven down to 120ºC for 45 minutes. Remove the meringues form the oven and allow to cool.

**4**

Using a melon ball tool, scoop various flavoured ice creams into small balls. Place in the middle of the macaroons and freeze until needed.

**5**

Once the meringue has cooled pipe a circle of whipped cream into the centre and place alternating macaroon shells around the edge of the base.

**6**

Carefully place the medium meringue on top of the bottom layer and add more filled macaroons. Pipe whipped cream onto the top macaroons. Decorate with raspberries and redcurrants.

# Chocolate Truffle Cake

## Ingredients

Square chocolate sponge cake (see page 15)

400 g / 14 oz / 1 ¾ cups chocolate ganache (see page 22)

110 g / 4 oz / 1 cup dark chocolate, melted

2 tbsp unsweetened cocoa powder

edible gold leaf

# SERVES 8 | PREP TIME 2 hours

Spread the melted dark chocolate onto a sheet of greaseproof paper and leave to set.

Use an ice cream scoop to form a ball of ganache and reserve.

Spread the rest of the ganache over the top and sides of the cake.

Dust the cake with cocoa powder.

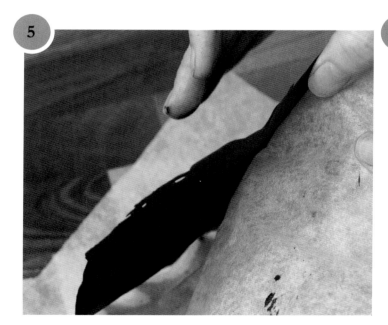

Carefully lift the chocolate sheet off of the greaseproof paper and break into shards.

Carefully stick the chocolate shards into the centre of the cake.

7

Dust the reserved ganache truffle with cocoa powder and set it in the centre of the chocolate shards.

8

Use a dry brush to apply the edible gold leaf to the truffle.

# Chocolate Orange Ribbon Cake

## Ingredients

110 g / 4 oz / 1 cup self-raising flour, sifted

110 g / 4 oz / ½ cup caster (superfine) sugar

110 g / 4 oz / ½ cup butter, softened

2 large eggs

2 tbsp orange zest, finely grated

150 g / 5 oz / 1 cup chocolate chips

1 chocolate girolle and cutter

225 g / 8 oz / 1 cup buttercream

## SERVES 16 | PREP TIME 3 hours | COOKING TIME 35 minutes

Preheat the oven to 190⁰C (170⁰ fan) / 375F / gas 5 and line a 20 cm/ 8" round tin with greaseproof paper. Prepare and measure all of the ingredients.

Combine the flour, sugar, butter, eggs and half of the orange zest in a bowl and whisk together for 2 minutes or until smooth, then fold in the chocolate chips.

**3**

Spoon the mixture into the tin and bake for 35 minutes. Once cooked, transfer the cakes to a wire rack and leave to cool completely.

**4**

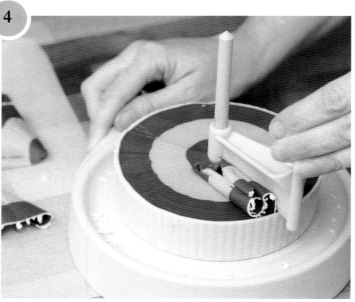

Use a chocolate roll cutting wheel to shave the chocolate girolle into delicate ribbons.

**5**

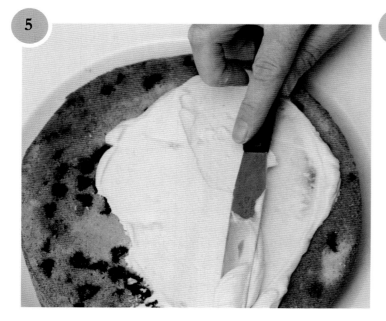

Spread the top of the cake with buttercream.

**6**

Sprinkle over the remaining orange zest.

7

Starting from the centre, stick the chocolate ribbons into the buttercream.

8

Continue to build up the layers until the whole of the top of the cake is covered and then spread out the chocolate ribbons.

# Chocolate Ice Cream Terrine

## Ingredients

500 ml / 17 fl. oz / 1 pint dark chocolate ice cream

300 ml / 10 ½ fl. oz / 1 ¼ cups milk chocolate ice cream

200 g / 7 oz dark chocolate, melted

110 g / 4 oz white chocolate, melted

edible gold leaf

## SERVES 6-8 | PREP TIME 2 hours

Spread ¾ of the dark chocolate over a piece of cellophane and use it to line a terrine mould.

Use the rest of the chocolate to coat thin strips of cellophane, then wrap them around a glass to form the ribbons. Leave the chocolate to set.

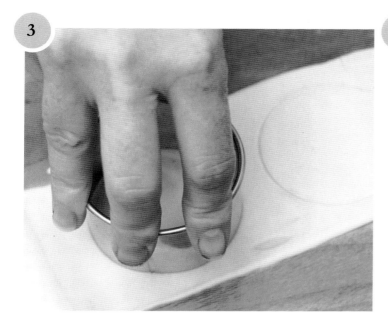

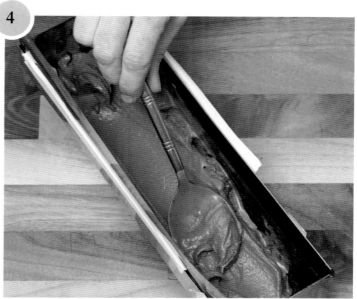

Spread the white chocolate over a piece of cellophane and leave to set. Cut it into rounds with a pastry cutter.

Fill the terrine with half of the dark chocolate ice cream and hollow out a channel in the centre.

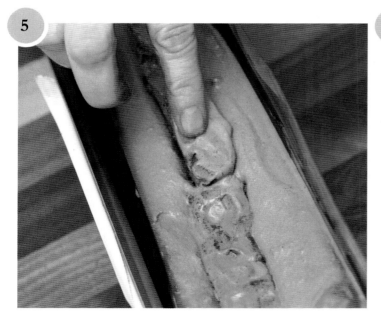

Fill with the milk chocolate ice cream, then top with the rest of the dark chocolate ice cream.

Freeze until firm and then turn out onto a serving plate. Decorate the terrine with the chocolate ribbons, white chocolate circles and gold leaf.

# Sugared Rose Cake

## Ingredients

Round vanilla sponge cake (see page 44)

icing sugar for dusting

1 egg white

handful of fresh rose petals

5 basil leaves

30 g / 1oz / ¼ cup caster (super fine) sugar

## SERVES 6 | PREP TIME 15 minutes

Trim the edges and top of the sponge cake.

Dust the top with a liberal amount of icing sugar.

Gently brush the rose petals with egg white. Then drag the petals through the caster sugar coating them thoroughly. Allow to dry.

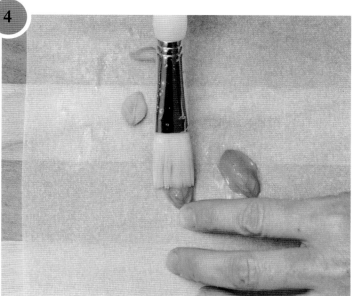

Gently brush the basil leaves with egg white.

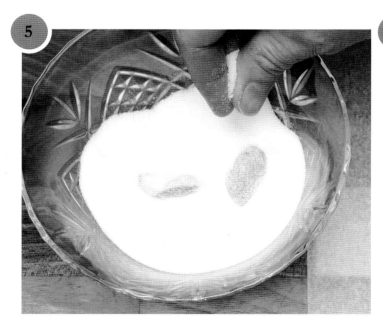

Drag the leaves through the caster sugar coating them thoroughly. Allow to dry.

Arrange the petals and leaves on the cake and serve.

# Chocolate and Raspberry Gateau

## Ingredients

Round chocolate sponge cake
(see page 15)
400 g / 14 oz / 1 ¾ cups chocolate ganache (see page 22)
200 g / 7 oz / 1 cup whipped cream
2 tbsp raspberry jam
200 g / 7 oz / 1 ¼ cups fresh raspberries
fresh mint leaves
icing sugar to dust

## SERVES 8 | PREP TIME 1 hour 30 minutes

Prepare and measure out all of the ingredients.

Fold 150 g / 5 oz of the chocolate ganache into the whipped cream. Cut the cake in half horizontally and sandwich together with the chocolate ganache.

Spread the rest of the ganache over the top and sides of the cake. Use a palette knife to give a smooth, even finish.

Spread the raspberry jam over the top of the cake.

Position the raspberries on top of the cake.

Tuck the mint leaves in and around the raspberries. Dust the cake lightly with icing sugar to finish.

# Cherry and Chocolate Cheesecake

## Ingredients

200 g / 7 oz / 1 cup granulated sugar

round chocolate sponge cake
(see page 15)

60 ml / 2 fl. oz / ¼ cup cherry syrup

150 g / 5 oz / 1 cup black cherries in syrup, drained

600 g / 1 lb 5 oz / 2 ½ cups cream cheese

150 ml / 5 fl. oz / ½ cup double cream

110 g / 4 oz / ½ cup caster (super fine) sugar

1 lemon, zest and juice

## SERVES 10 | PREP TIME 1 hour

Prepare and measure all of the ingredients.

Put the sugar in a heavy bottomed saucepan and heat until it starts to melt around the edges. Gently swirl the pan over the heat until it has all melted. Pour the caramel onto a non-stick baking mat. Leave to cool and harden.

Put the cake into a loose-bottomed plastic cake mould that fits exactly and brush with the cherry syrup.

Space ¾ of the cherries out on top of the cake.

Beat the cream cheese with the cream, sugar and lemon zest and juice and spoon over the cherries. Spread the mixture out with a palette knife and chill for 2 hours.

Take the cake out of the mould and transfer to a serving plate.

**7**

Top with the reserved cherries.

**8**

Smash the cooled caramel with a rolling pin.

**9**

Stick the shards into the top of the cheesecake.

# Kiwi and Almond Cake

## Ingredients

Vanilla sponge cake, loaf-shaped
(see page 14)

500 g / 17 oz / 1 ¾ cups buttercream

1 tsp almond essence

40 g / 1 ½ oz / ¼ cup ground almonds

4 kiwi fruit, peeled and sliced

15 raspberries

coloured balls

metallic leaves for decoration

## SERVES 8 | PREP TIME 1 hour 30 minutes

Measure and prepare all of the ingredients.

Whip the buttercream with the almond essence and ground almond.

3

Slice the sponge loaf and spread with the almond buttercream using a palette knife.

4

Carefully sandwich the sponges loaves together.

5

Coat the cake with more of the almond cream.

Place the kiwi slices onto the sides and top of the cake.

Position the silver leaves onto the top of the cake.

Decorate with the raspberries and coloured balls.

# Gooseberry, Peach and White Chocolate Cake

## Ingredients

Round Victoria sponge filled with apricot
jam (see page 18)
1 punnet of Cape gooseberries (physalis)
2 firm peaches
1 small orange
400 g / 14 oz / 1 ¾ cups  buttercream
125 g / 4 ½ / 1 cup white chocolate
coloured cocoa collar transfer

## SERVES 4 | PREP TIME 1 hour 30 minutes

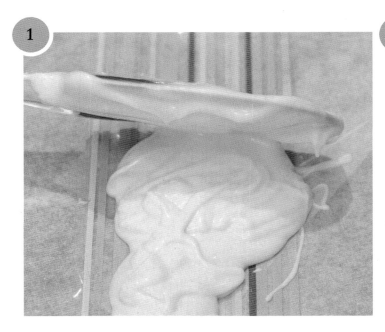

Melt the white chocolate gently over a bain-marie. When melted, spread the chocolate over the back of the cocoa transfer.

Crumb coat the cake with buttercream, ensuring even coverage. Next, wrap the transfer around the cake carefully. Place in the refrigerator to chill and set.

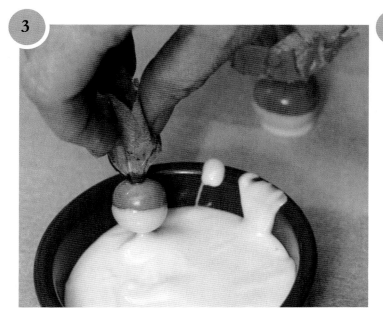

Meanwhile dip the Cape gooseberries into the white chocolate and allow to set on greaseproof paper.

When the chocolate has hardened, carefully remove the acetate backing from the transfer to leave the pattern showing.

Using a zesting tool, make some fine orange peel. Arrange the cape gooseberries across the top of the cake.

Slice the peaches into thin wedges and arrange amongst the Cape gooseberries. Scatter with fine orange peel and serve.

# Chocolate Ganache and Raspberry Gateau

## Ingredients

3 chocolate sponge cakes
(see page 15)
400 g / 14 oz dark chocolate, melted
350 ml / 12 fl. oz / 1 ½ cups double cream,
whipped
110 g / 4 oz white chocolate shards
150 g / 5 oz / 1 cup raspberries
icing sugar to dust

**SERVES 10 | PREP TIME 1 hour**

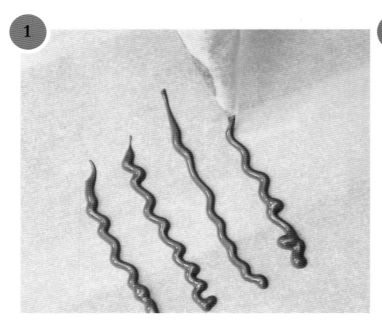

Spoon 50 g of the melted chocolate into a small piping bag and pipe squiggles onto a sheet of greaseproof paper. Leave to set.

Fold the rest of the melted chocolate into the whipped cream and spoon the mixture into a piping bag. Pipe large beads of the ganache onto the first cake to fill the entire surface (see pages 26-27).

Top with the second cake and repeat the beading to use up another third of the ganache.

Top with the third cake and pipe the rest of the ganache on top. Stud the cake with raspberries.

Position the white chocolate shards between the raspberries. Use a palette knife to lift the chocolate squiggles off the paper and transfer them carefully to the cake.

Dust the cake with a little icing sugar to finish.

# Chocolate Yule Log

## Ingredients

Chocolate log cake (see page 19)

2 tbsp unsweetened cocoa powder

1 tbsp icing sugar

110 g / 4 oz / ½ cup dark chocolate fondant
icing (see pages 28-29)

200 g / 7 oz dark chocolate, melted

## SERVES 8 | PREP TIME 2 hours

Dust the log generously with cocoa powder. Sprinkle the top with a little icing sugar.

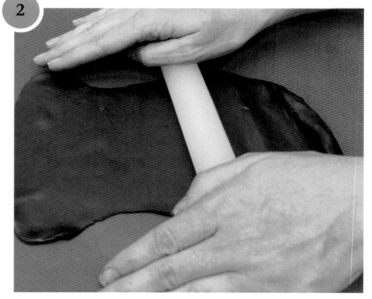

Knead the chocolate fondant icing until pliable, then roll out on a non-stick mat.

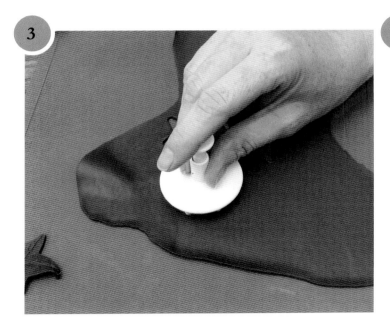

Use an ivy leaf plunger cutter to cut out the ivy leaves.

Roll the trimmings into thin sticks and pine needles with a cake smoother. Pile the sticks and pine needles on top of the log. Arrange the ivy leaves in amongst the sticks.

Pour the melted chocolate onto a marble slab and spread it out with a palette knife. Leave to set. Use a wallpaper stripper to make chocolate curls.

Carefully arrange them onto the cake. Dust with a little more icing sugar to finish.

# Christmas Fruit Cake

## Ingredients

Round fruit cake, iced with white fondant
(see page 16 and 28-29)
200 g / 7 oz / 1 cup marzipan (see pages 30-31)
green food dye
orange food dye
red food dye
brown food dye
copper food dust

## SERVES 8 | PREP TIME 2 hours

Divide and colour the marzipan using the food colours. Roll out the green marzipan and cut out ivy and holly leaves using leaf cutters. Shape the leaves and allow to firm.

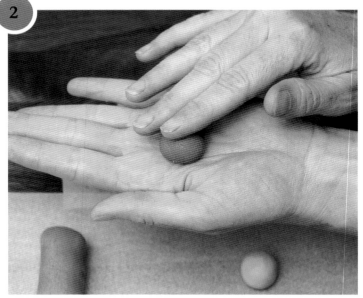

Make balls using the orange and green marzipan. Take the orange balls and roll over a sieve to make indentations.

**3**

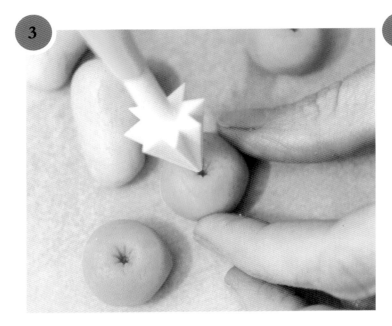

Using a serrated tapered cone tool, mark the bottom side of the green ball to make an apple shape.

**4**

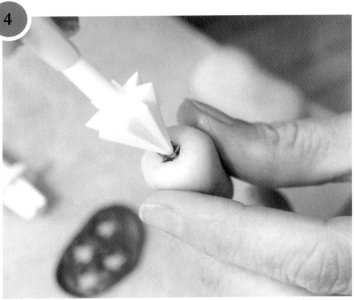

To make the pears, roll a green ball between two fingers to form the shape and use the cone tool to create the base of the pear. Make stalks using the brown marzipan and fix onto the apples and pears.

**5**

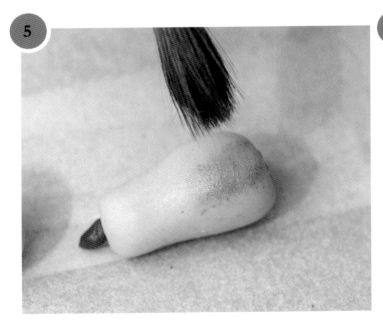

Roll a small amount of green marzipan and using a small petal cutter, create the stalk for the orange. Apply a light dusting of the copper dust to the pear to create a blush effect.

**6**

Create holly berries by rolling a number of small balls from red marzipan. Arrange the fruit and leaves onto the top of the cake and tie a ribbon around the base.

# Yellow Ribbons and Roses Wedding Cake

## Ingredients

1 x 30 cm / 12" round vanilla sponge cake
(see page 14)

1 x 23 cm / 9" round sponge cake
(see page 14)

1 x 15 cm / 6" round chocolate sponge cake
(see page 15)

2.5 kg / 5 ½ lbs / 11 cups yellow fondant
icing (see pages 28-29)

300 g / 10 oz / 1 ⅓ cups royal icing

edible lustre (optional) (see page 23)

200 g / 7 oz / ¾ cup sugar florist paste

green food colouring

500 g / 1 lb 1 oz / 2 ½ cups Isomalt

55 g / 2 oz / 3 tbsp liquid glucose

pink food colouring

## SERVES 25 | PREP TIME 3 hours

Prepare and measure all of the ingredients.

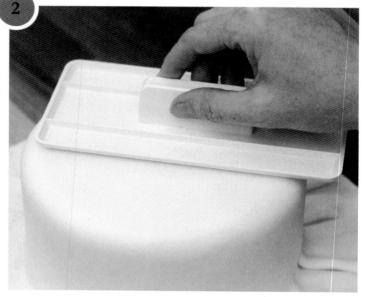

Cover each cake with fondant icing, using a cake smoother to get a smooth, professional finish. Trim away any excess icing. Stack the cakes on top of each other, securing with a little royal icing.

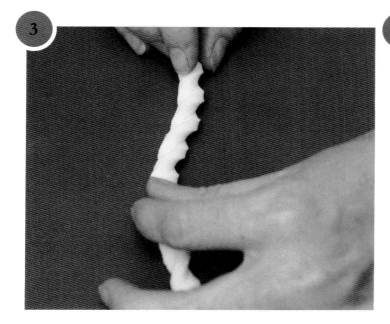

Use a pump action sugarcraft gun to extrude a long strip of fondant icing. Fold the strip in half and twist to form a rope.

Draw a lace pattern onto tracing paper and transfer the design to the side of the cake by pricking through the paper. Use white royal icing to pipe over the design.

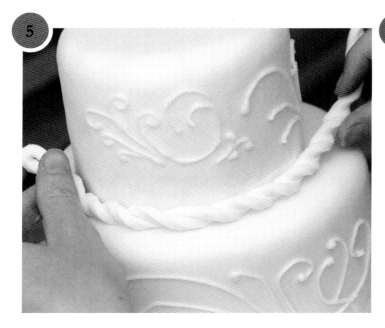

Use the fondant rope to hide the join between the cakes, securing with a little royal icing.

To make the rose petals, use your fingers to flatten out small balls of florist paste. Thin the petals using a ball tool and a foam pad.

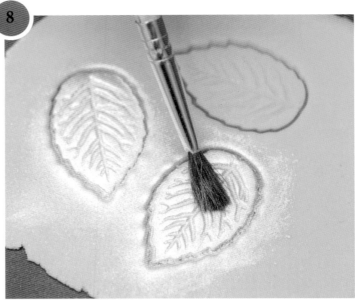

Assemble the roses using water or flower glue to attach. Leave the roses to harden for 24 hours before brushing with edible lustre.

Colour the remaining sugar paste with a little green food colouring. Roll it out as thin as possible and use a rose leaf cutter to cut out the leaves. Dust with edible lustre and leave to harden for 24 hours over scrunched foil to give a natural shape.

To make the ribbons, stir the Isomalt over a low heat until the crystals dissolve. Add the glucose and boil. Add a little pink food colouring, then pour onto an oiled marble slab to cool. Put small pieces of the cooled Isomalt under a heat lamp. When pliable, pull each piece until thin.

Bend the sugar ribbon round into a loop. Pinch away any excess paste and repeat to form the rest of the ribbon loops. Assemble the pulled sugar ribbons on top of the cake, and decorate the lower tiers with the roses and leaves.

# White Chocolate Wedding Cake

## Ingredients

3 square fondant iced sponge cakes in
decreasing sizes (4", 6" and 8")
(see pages 14 and 28-29)
1 kg / 2.2 lbs / 10 cups white chocolate
fresh hydrangeas
1" in / 2.5 cm thick polystyrene blocks
florists wire
cream satin ribbon

## SERVES 10-15 | PREP TIME 1 hour 25 minutes

Very gently melt the white chocolate over a Bain-Marie, making sure that
the water doesn't touch the bottom of the bowl. Stir continuously until
melted. Pour the white chocolate onto a marble slab.

Using a pallet knife spread the chocolate and allow to cool until almost
hard. Score lines in the chocolate, 8cm apart. Push a sharp slightly oiled
blade, at a low angle, across the chocolate to create long uniform rolls.

107

Place the cakes onto cake boards (each one slightly larger than the cakes. Coat the sides of the cakes in melted white chocolate.

Stick the rolls to the sides of all of the cakes.

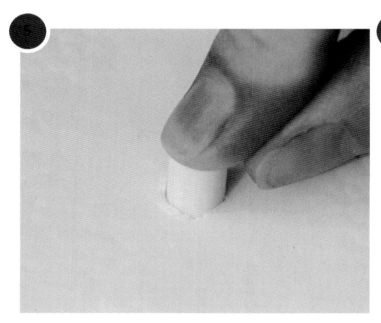

Push support dowels into the bottom and middle tiers of the cake.

Using melted chocolate, stick cigarillos to the boards of the cake. When set, surround the cake boards with cream ribbon.

Trim the hydrangea stems and insert short lengths of wire into the stems leaving about 3 cm of wire sticking out of the end of each blossom.

Place a polystyrene block on the top of the bottom tier ensuring it rests on the dowels.

Push the wired hydrangeas into the polystyrene around the cake tier. Place the second tier onto the polystyrene block and repeat the last stage. Top with hydrangeas to complete the cake.

# Chocolate Rosebud Cake

## Ingredients

round chocolate sponge cake
(see page 15)

110 g / 2 oz dark chocolate, melted

1 kg / 2 lbs 3 oz / 4 ½ cups dark chocolate
fondant icing (see pages 28-29)

16 fresh roses

1 egg white, beaten

55 g / 2 oz / ¼ cup caster (superfine) sugar

1 tsp pink dusting powder

## SERVES 8 | PREP TIME 1 hour

Spread the cake with melted chocolate.

Cover with fondant icing, using a cake smoother to get a smooth, professional finish. Trim away any excess icing.

Remove the stalks from the roses.

Brush the roses with egg white.

Mix the caster sugar with the pink dusting powder and sprinkle onto the roses until they are completely covered, shaking off any excess.

Attach the roses to the cake with a little more melted chocolate.

# Pink Fairy Cake

## Ingredients

round vanilla sponge cake (see page 14)

250 g / 8 oz / 1 cup flesh coloured fondant (see pages 28-29)

500 g / 16 oz / 2 cups pink fondant (see pages 28-29)

125 g / 4 oz / ½ cup white fondant (see pages 28-29)

60 g / 2 oz / ¼ cup yellow fondant (see pages 28-29)

glitter piping gel

edible glue

## SERVES 8 | PREP TIME 1 hour 30 minutes

To make the fairy, roll a small amount of flesh coloured fondant into a ball for the head, a very small ball for the nose, two lengths for the arms and two balls for the feet.

Make a mouth by gently pushing the edge of a piping nozzle into the face. Stick on the fairy's nose and mark two eyes using and edible icing pen. Then form the fairy body using pink fondant.

112

**3**

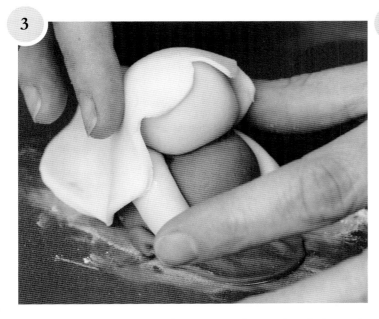

Roll out some yellow fondant and cut out a star shape to form the hair and glue to the fairy's head.

**4**

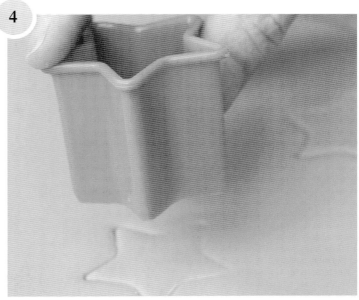

Using a rolling pin, roll out the pink and white fondant. Take a star shape cutter and cut out white and pink stars and set aside. Make star indents on the surface of the cake.

**5**

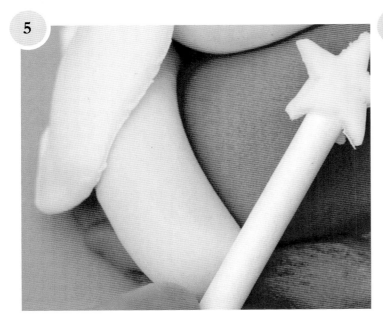

Arrange the fairy on the cake and cut a short length of a lollypop stick to create the fairy wand. Using edible glue stick on the yellow stars to the lollypop stick.

**6**

Using royal icing or edible glue fix the stars to the cake. Pipe the glitter gel onto the centre of the stars.

# Yellow Chick Cake

## Ingredients

round vanilla cake (see page 14)

1 kg / 35 oz / 4 ½ cups yellow fondant (see pages 28-29)

30 g / 1 oz / ⅛ cup orange fondant (see pages 28-29)

15 g / ½ oz / ¹/₁₆ cup white fondant (see pages 28-29)

green 25 cm / 10 inch cake board

## SERVES 8-10 | PREP TIME 1 hour 35 minutes

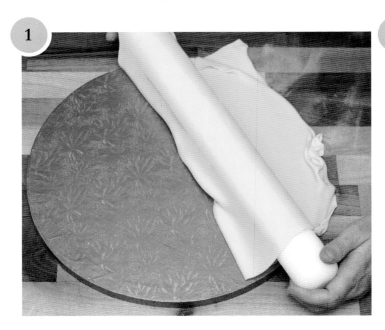

Line a cake board with yellow fondant.

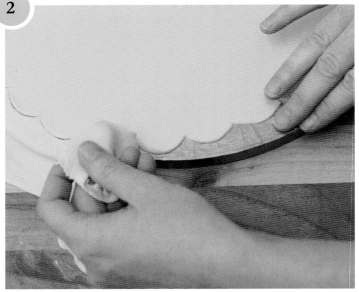

Using a circle cutter, cut away semi-circles to make a scalloped edge.

**3**

Cover the sponge in buttercream and place in the refrigerator to set. Once set, cover the cake using yellow fondant and set aside to harden.

**4**

Roll a large ball of yellow fondant and then flatten slightly using the cake smoother.

**5**

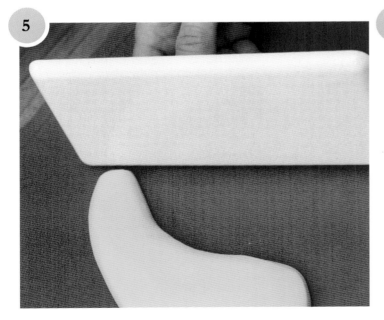

Make the wings by rolling out a length of yellow fondant into a long egg shape. Cut this piece in half to make 2 wings. Flatten slightly using a cake smoother.

**6**

Now make small diamond shape out of orange fondant and using a knife push down into the fondant to form a beak.

**7**

Roll out two small circles out of white fondant and allow to dry. Once dry, draw on the pupils using an edible icing pen. Arrange the beak and eyes on the face. Place the wings and face on top of the cake.

**8**

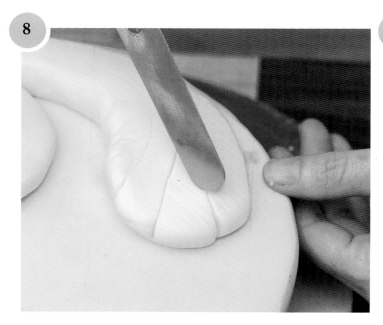

Using a small palette knife, make indentations to mimic feathers on the wings and face.

**9**

Fix a green ribbon around the base of the cake using double sided adhesive tape.

# Wedding Cake

## Ingredients

20 cm / 8" round vanilla sponge cake
(see page 14)

25 cm / 10" round vanilla sponge cake
(see page 14)

400 g / 1 lb / 1 ¾ cups buttercream

2 kg / 4 lbs / 9 cups white fondant icing (see
pages 28-29)

200 g / 7 oz / ¾ cup royal icing (see page 23)

### For Decoration

ribbon

flowers

bride and groom models

pillars

dowels

2 cake boards, 1 medium, 1 large

## SERVES 4 | PREP TIME 2 hours

Take the two sponge cakes, one larger than the other and crumb coat in
buttercream.

Cover the cake with white fondant, smooth out with cake smoothers to
obtain an even finish. Trim the cakes and stick them to two cake boards
with a little buttercream.

**3**

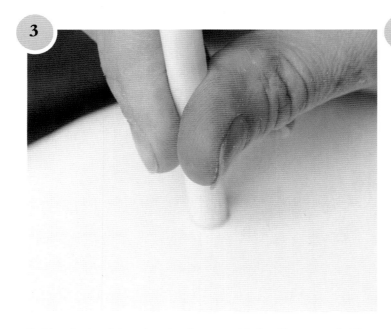

Position the dowels into the cake where you wish the pillars to stand. Allow the fondant to harden.

**4**

With a medium width star piping nozzle, pipe royal icing swirls around the tops of the cakes.

**5**

With a medium width star piping nozzle, pipe royal icing in a scallop pattern around the cake bottoms where the meet the boards.

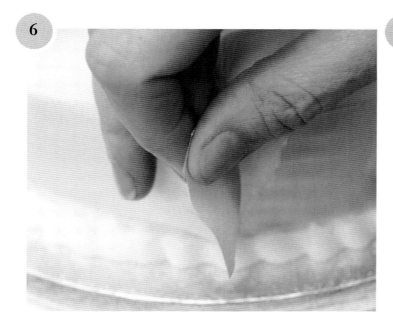

Tie a ribbon around the top and bottom tier of the cake above the scallop piping.

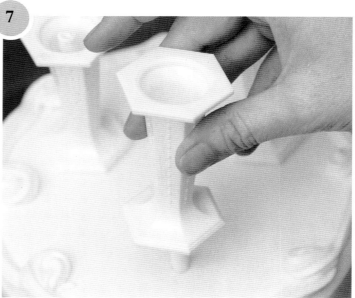

Thread the pillar supports over the dowels.

Place the smaller cake and board on top to the pillars.

Place the bride and groom and any other decorations on the top tier and place the flowers onto the top and bottom tiers of the cake.

# First Birthday Cake

## Ingredients

75 g / 2 ½ oz / ⅓ cup pink fondant icing (see pages 28-29)

1 x 20 cm / 8" chocolate sponge cake
(see page 15)

1 x 8 cm / 3"square vanilla sponge cake
(see page 14)

300 g / 10 ½ oz / ⅓ cups buttercream

mixed sweets

strawberry liquorice

mini marshmallows

number 1 candle

**SERVES** 16 | **PREP TIME** 1 hour

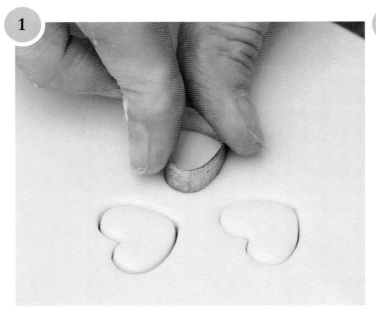

Roll out the fondant icing and use a small heart-shaped cutter to cut out icing hearts.

Spread the top and sides of the cake with buttercream and use the palette knife to make small peaks in the icing. Top with the small square cake and cover with buttercream.

**3**

Decorate the top of the main cake with sweets.

**4**

Decorate the edges of the cake with short lengths of strawberry liquorice interspersed with mini marshmallows.

**5**

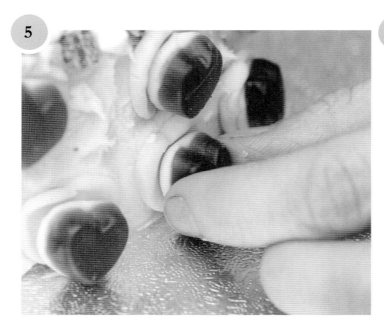

Press the icing hearts around the side of the cake. Use a little buttercream to stick heart-shaped sweets in the centre of the icing hearts. Add a second row of icing and sweet hearts round the bottom of the cake.

**6**

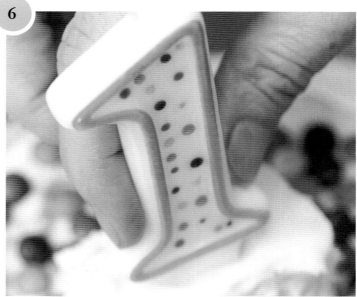

Decorate the edge of the board with more sweets before topping the cake with the number one candle.

# Gold Ribbon Cake

## Ingredients

round cake with white fondant
(see pages 14 and 28-29)
500 g / 17 oz / 2 cups white fondant (see pages 28-29)
100 g / 3½ oz / ½ cup royal icing (see page 23)
gold leaf
gold ribbons

## SERVES 4-6 | PREP TIME 1 hour

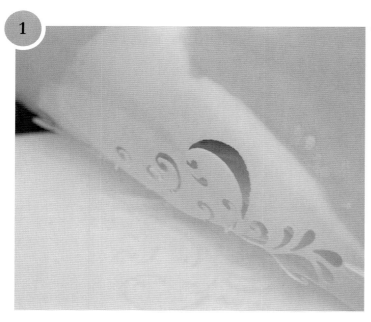

Using a stencil and flat side scraper tool, scrape the royal icing over the top
of the cake and allow to dry.

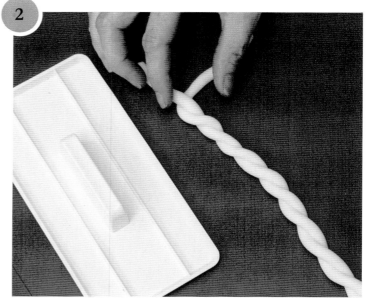

Form a rope by twisting a single length of white fondant and stick in swags
around the cake.

**3**

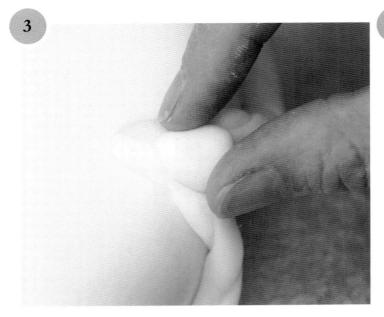

At the top of each swag, stick a pearl drop shaped piece of fondant on the cake.

**4**

Using a craft knife or small paint brush apply gold leaf to the pearl drops.

**5**

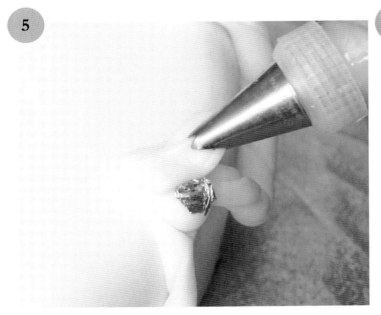

Using a leaf nozzle, pipe two royal icing leaf shapes onto the pearl drops and rope swags.

**6**

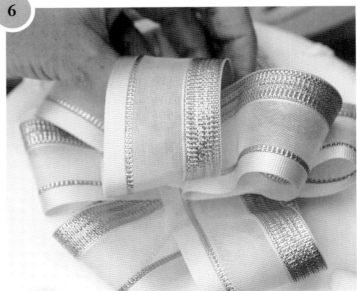

Fix ribbon around the base of the cake. Tie a bow in a ribbon and place this on the top of the cake.

# Mini Rose Cake

## Ingredients

1 x 8 cm / 3"square vanilla sponge cake
(see page 14)
55 g / 2 oz / ¼ cup buttercream
110 g / 4 oz / ½ cup white fondant icing (see pages 28-29)
55 g / 2 oz / ¼ cup red fondant icing (see pages 28-29)
55 g / 2 oz / ¼ cup green royal icing  (see pages 28-29)
red ribbon

## SERVES 1 | PREP TIME 1 hour

Spread the top and the sides of the cake with buttercream.

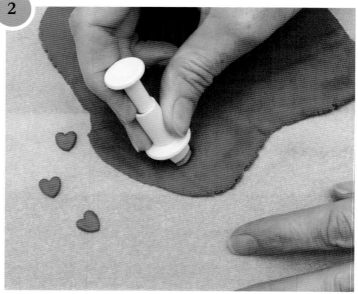

Roll out the red fondant icing and cut out 4 small hearts.

Use the rest of the fondant to make the roses. Flatten small balls of the paste between cellophane and use to make the petals.

Assemble the roses with a dab of water.

Knead the white fondant then roll out on a work surface that has been lightly dusted with icing sugar.

Use the rolling pin to transfer the icing to the cake and mould it down and around the sides.

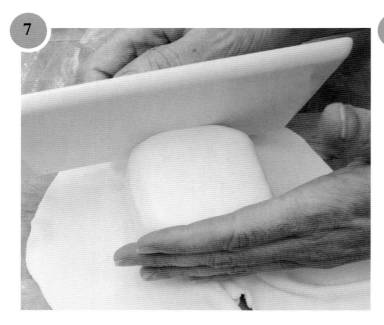

Use a cake smoother to get a smooth, professional finish to the icing.

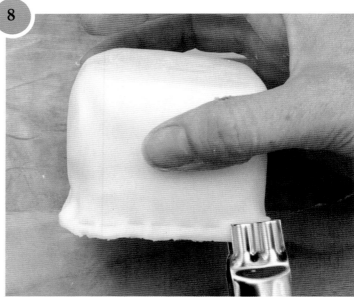

Use a crimping tool to scallop the bottom edge of the icing.

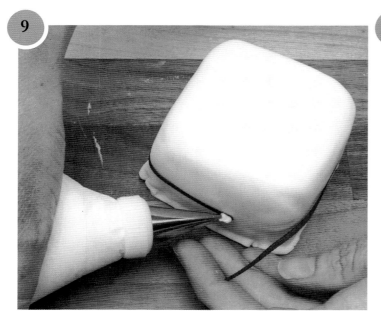

Wrap the ribbon around the cake, attaching with a small blob of icing.

Pipe 3 leaves onto the top of the cake with the royal icing. Attach the roses and hearts with a small blob of icing.

# Coffee and Cream Wedding Cake

## Ingredients

3 kg / 6 lbs 8 oz / 13 cups fondant icing
(see pages 28-29)

brown food colouring

1 x 40 cm / 16" round vanilla sponge cake
(see page 14)

1 x 20 cm / 8" round vanilla sponge cake
(see page 14)

1 x 15 cm / 6" round chocolate sponge cake
(see page 15)

600 g / 1 lb 5 oz / 2 ½ cups royal icing
(see page 23)

sugared almonds

sugar pearls

silver dragees

## SERVES 60 | PREP TIME 3 hours

Prepare and measure all of the ingredients.

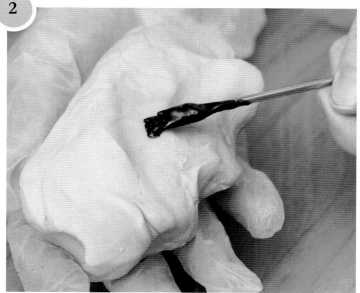

Colour the fondant icing with the brown food colouring, kneading well to remove any streaks.

**3**

Roll out and cover each cake with fondant icing, using a cake smoother to get a smooth, professional finish. Trim away any excess icing. Stack the cakes on top of each other, securing with a little royal icing.

**4**

Use a pastry cutter to gently mark the edges of the cake as a guide for the royal icing.

**5**

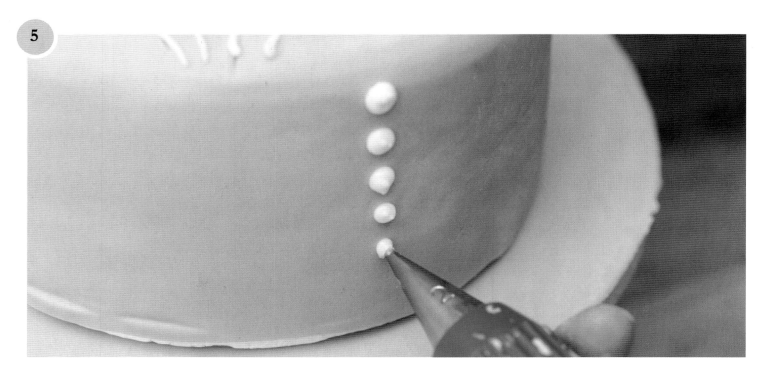

Using the indentations as a guide, use the royal icing to pipe swags around the cake. Pipe beads of royal icing between the swags.

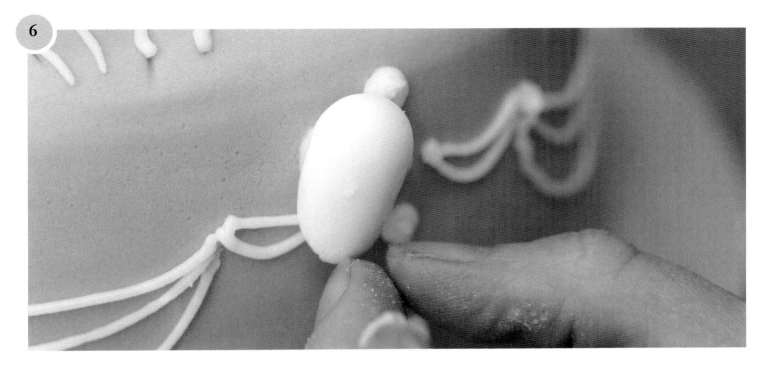

Attach the sugared almonds, pearls and dragees to the cake with a little royal icing.

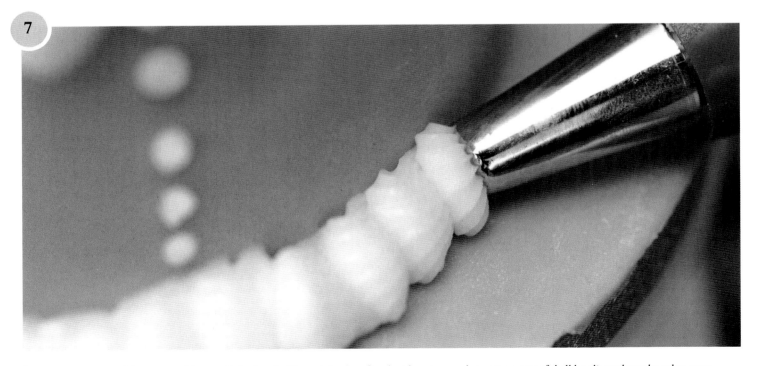

Dust away any excess icing sugar with a small dry brush. Use a piping bag fitted with a star nozzle to pipe a row of shell beading where the cakes meet.

# Pink Jungle Wedding Cake

## Ingredients

1 x 30 cm / 12" round vanilla sponge cake
(see page 14)

1 x 23 cm / 9" round vanilla sponge cake
(see page 14)

1 x 15 cm / 6" round chocolate sponge cake
(see page 15)

2.5 kg / 5 ½ lbs / 11 cups pink fondant icing
(see page 28-29)

300 g / 10 oz / 1 ⅓ royal icing (see page 23)

200 g / 7 oz / ¾ cup sugar florist paste

green food colouring

500 g / 1 lb 1 oz / 2 ½ cups Isomalt

55 g / 2 oz / 3 tbsp liquid glucose

pink food colouring

**SERVES 25 | PREP TIME 3 hours decorating time**

Prepare and measure all of the ingredients.

Cover each cake with fondant icing, using a cake smoother to get a smooth, professional finish. Trim away any excess icing. Stack the cakes on top of each other, securing with a little royal icing.

**3**

To make the rose petals, flatten small balls of florist paste and thin into petals using a ball tool and a foam pad. Assemble the roses using water or flower glue to attach. For leaves, colour some sugar paste green and cut into leaf shapes. Leave roses and leaves to harden for 24 hours before brushing with edible lustre.

**4**

Use a pastry cutter to gently mark the edges of the cake as a guide for the royal icing. Using the indentations as a guide, use the royal icing to pipe swags around the cake. Pipe royal icing stars between the swags. Pipe a string of royal icing shells around the bottom of each cake where they join each other.

**5**

To make the ribbons, stir the Isomalt over a low heat until the crystals dissolve. Add the glucose and boil the mixture to 180°C. Add a little pink food colouring, then pour onto an oiled marble slab to cool. Put small pieces of the cooled Isomalt under a heat lamp. When pliable, pull each piece until thin and form into loops.

**6**

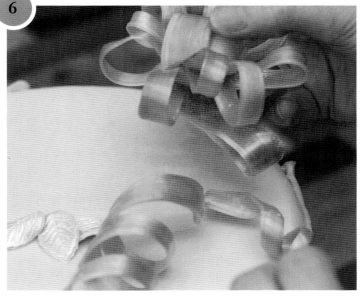

Repeat to form the rest of the ribbon loops. Assemble the pulled sugar ribbons on top of the cake, and decorate with the roses and leaves.

# Topsy Turvy Wedding Cake

## Ingredients

1 x 30 cm / 12" vanilla sponge cake
(see page 14)

1 x 23 cm / 9" vanilla sponge cake
(see page 14)

1 x 15 cm / 6" vanilla sponge cake
(see page 14)

450 g / 1 lb / 2 cups buttercream
(see page 23)

2 ½ kg / 5 ½ lbs / 11 cups fondant icing
purple food colouring
orange food colouring

## SERVES 40 | PREP TIME 4 hours

Use a bread knife to cut the tops off the cakes at an angle.

Use a palette knife to spread the cakes with 400 g of the buttercream.

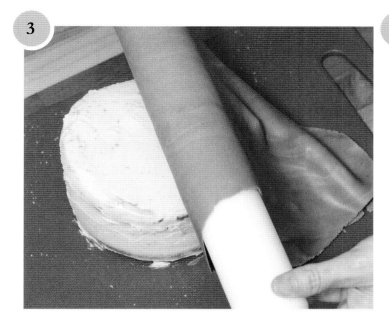

**3**

Colour 200 g of the icing orange and put on one side. Colour half of the remaining icing purple and use to cover the small and medium cake, using a cake smoother to get a smooth, professional finish. Trim away any excess icing.

**4**

Cover the large cake with white fondant icing. Then, roll out the orange fondant icing along with the white and purple icing trimmings. Cut out flowers with different sized flower cutters and attach to the side of the cakes with a dab of water.

**5**

Use a length of plastic dowel to secure the cakes together as you stack them on top of each other.

**6**

Colour the remaining buttercream orange and pipe a line round the bottom of the cakes where they join each other.

# Peach Wedgewood Celebration Cake

## Ingredients

1 x 30 cm / 12" square chocolate sponge cake
(see page 15)
2 kg / 4 lbs 5 oz / 9 cups fondant icing
peach food colouring (see pages 28-29)
300 g / 10 oz / 1 ⅓ cups royal icing (see page 23)

## SERVES 30 | PREP TIME 3 hours

Prepare and measure out all ingredients.

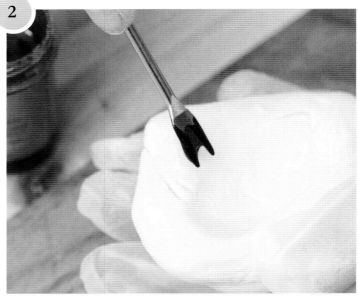

Colour the fondant icing with the food colouring, kneading well to remove any streaks.

**3**

Cover the cake with fondant icing, using a cake smoother to get a smooth, professional finish. Trim away any excess icing.

**4**

Pipe a line of royal icing down each corner of the cake.

**5**

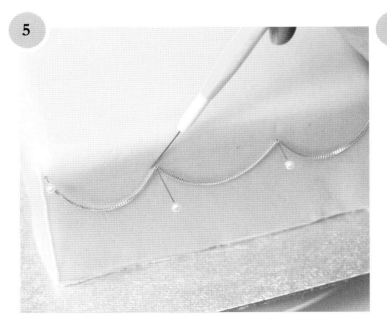

Using pins and a piece of string or chain mark out where you will ice the swags.

**6**

Pipe over the indentations with royal icing.

**7**

Pipe a second icing swag underneath each original one. Pipe a bow between and 6 small beads below each swag.

**8**

Pipe a line of beading around the top the cake. Continue to build up the lines of beading, being careful to keep the lines as straight and uniform as possible.

**9**

Pipe a line of icing to border the beading. Finally, pipe a joined-up row of beading around the base of the cake where it meets the board.

# Peach Wedding Cake

## Ingredients

3 circular vanilla sponge cakes in decreasing
sizes (6", 8" and 10") (see page 14)

500 g /1 lb 3 oz / 2 ¼ cups buttercream

200 g / 7oz / 2 cups royal icing (see page 23)

2 kg / 4 ½lbs / 10 cups white fondant icing
(see page 28-29)

peach food dye

# SERVES 10 | PREP TIME 1 hour 25 minutes

Cover the sponges with buttercream.

Cover with rolled white fondant and trim.

**3**

Using the cake smoothers, smooth out any blemishes. Use a little icing sugar if the fondant sticks.

**4**

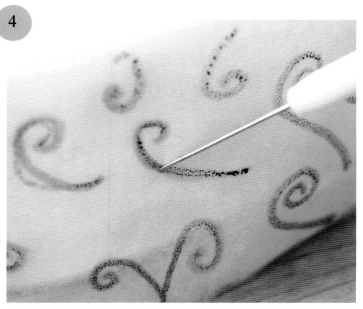

Draw scroll patterns onto baking paper. Place the template against the cake. Using a scribing tool, carefully mark out the pattern you wish to pipe onto the surface.

**5**

Colour some white fondant with peach coloured food colouring and roll into 3mm thick sheet. Cut a strip about 1.5 cm wide and about 12cm long.

**6**

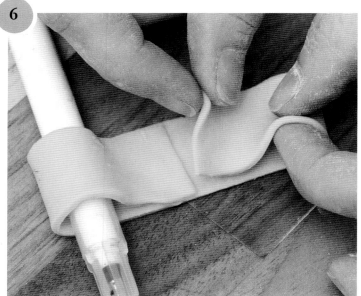

Take a clean pen about a third of the way in from each end. Roll the fondant back over the pens until they meet to create a bow shape. Seal the ends down with some edible glue.

**7**

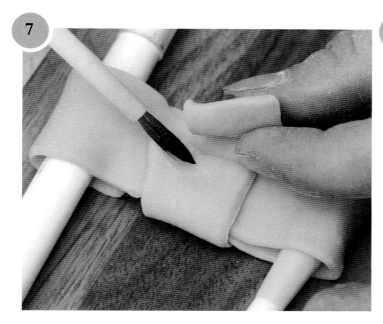

Take a shorter strip about 3 cm long and wrap this around the middle of the bow to make a loop, then stick down with edible glue. Make between 12-15 loops and leave to one side to harden.

**8**

Meanwhile colour some royal icing with peach food colouring. Using a small round piping nozzle pipe onto your scribed pattern around the sides and tops of the cakes.

**9**

Using a round nozzle pipe beads around the bottom of the cake where it meets the board. Repeat this around each cake tier.

**10**

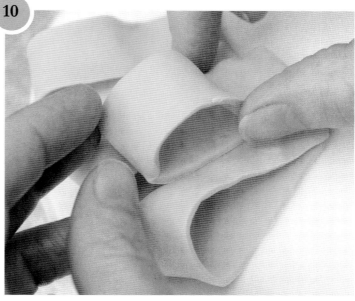

Arrange the bow components into a bow shape on the top of the cake and stick them down with edible glue. Allow to dry and then serve.

# Springtime Nut Cake

## Ingredients

6" vanilla sponge cake (see page 14)

250 g / 9 oz / 1 ¼ cups buttercream

100 g / 3.5 oz / ¾ cup chopped roasted mixed nuts

250 g / 9 oz / 1 ¼ cups fondant (see page 28-29)

50 g / 1.7 oz / ¼ cup royal icing (see page 23)

paste food colours: green, pink, yellow, lilac

## SERVES 6 | PREP TIME 1 hour

Prepare and measure out all the ingredients. Using the food colouring, tint the fondant to make four different shades.

Roll out the fondants. Cut out and mould flowers and butterflies and allow to dry.

**3**

Coat the sponge in buttercream using a palette knife.

**4**

Gently pat the side of the cake with the chopped nuts to coat. Continue this around the entire side of the cake.

**5**

Using a cake comb make a circular pattern in the top of the cake.

**6**

Arrange the flowers on top of the cake. Pipe stems using green royal icing.

# Star Cupcakes Chocolate Cake

## Ingredients

20 cm / 8" round vanilla sponge (see page 14)
8 cm / 3" round vanilla sponge (see page 14)
5 chocolate cupcakes (see page 14)
1 ¼ kg / 2 ¾ lbs / 6 cups white fondant
(see pages 28-29)
400 g / 14 oz / 1 ¾ cups vanilla buttercream
50 g / 1.7 oz / ¼ cup chocolate fondant (see pages 28-29)
150 g / 5 oz / ¾ cup blue fondant (see pages 28-29)

## SERVES 8-10 | PREP TIME 1 hour 30 minutes

Cover a cake board with blue fondant and allow to harden

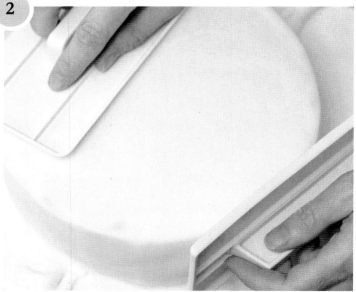

Cover the two sponges in buttercream and chill. Roll out 1kg of the fondant and cover both sponges. Smooth the fondant and set the cakes aside to harden.

**3**

To make the decorations, roll out the chocolate and blue fondant and use star shaped cutters to cut out stars in various sizes.

**4**

Place the remaining buttercream in a piping bag with a large star nozzle and pipe swirls onto the cupcakes. Decorate the cupcakes with some of the fondant stars.

**5**

Using edible glue stick the fondant stars onto the sponges in a random pattern.

**6**

Place the larger cake onto the cake board and stack the smaller sponge on top. Fix a ribbon around the base of the bottom cake and arrange the cupcakes on top of the bottom tier.

# Pink Heart Fondant Cake

## Ingredients

2 heart vanilla sponge cakes 1 medium one small (see page 14)

buttercream icing (see pages 28-29)

200 g / 7 oz / 1 cup apricot jam

100 g / 3 ½ oz / ½ cup red fondant (see pages 28-29)

50 g / 1 ¾ oz / ¼ cup green fondant (see pages 28-29)

50 g / 1 ¾ oz / ¼ cup white fondant (see pages 28-29)

1 ½ kg / 2 ¾ lbs / 5 cups light pink fondant (see pages 28-29)

250 g / 9oz / 1 ¼ cup dark pink fondant (see pages 28-29)

## SERVES 8 | PREP TIME 45 minutes

Slice the cakes in half, horizontally. Spread the bottom half with buttercream and the top half with jam. Then sandwich the two halves together.

Roll out the fondant to cover cake board. Brush the cake board lightly with water to moisten. Using a rolling pin, lift the fondant and lay onto the board.

3

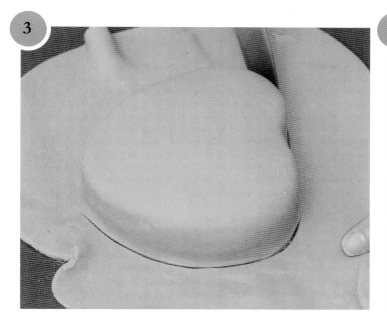

Use a sharp knife to trim the excess. Cover 2 heart cakes with the pink fondant and allow the fondant to harden.

4

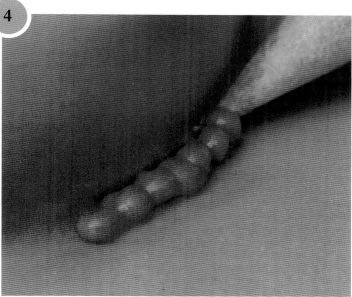

Stack the cakes centrally onto the board. Pipe around the base of each tier using a snail trail pattern.

5

Make a fondant wrap for the bottom tier. Roll out the red fondant icing and stamp a border cutter into the icing. Carefully slice along the bottom.

6

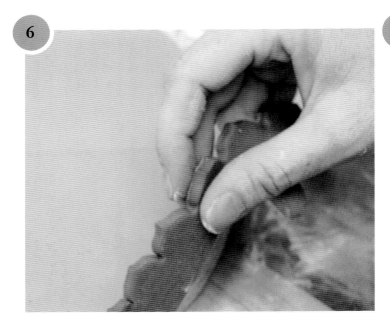

Stick the fondant wrap around the iced board using the royal icing to glue.

7

Stamp out some leaves from the green fondant and create some roses using the red fondant.

8

Position roses and hearts and stick using edible glue or a small amount of royal icing and allow to set.

# White and Blue Fondant Bow Cake

## Ingredients

4" (11 cm) cubed sponge cake covered in
white fondant (see page 14 and pages 28-29)
250 g / 8 oz / 1 ¼ cups packet light blue
fondant icing (see pages 28-29)
icing sugar for dusting

## SERVES 4 | PREP TIME 1 hour

Using marzipan spacers roll out the light blue fondant to a width of 3 cm
on a sheet of greaseproof paper lightly dusted with icing sugar. Cut four 13
cm x 3 cm strips using a pizza cutter or sharp knife.

Re-roll the remaining fondant using the spacers to a length of 30cm x 4cm
wide. Cut into three equal lengths with a sharp knife.

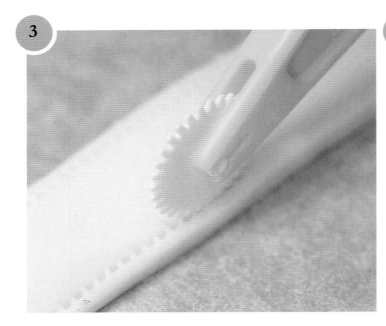

Using a wheel tool, mark along the edges of each piece of fondant to give a stitching effect.

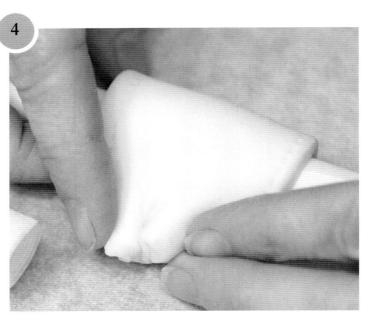

Roll two of the 10cm x 4cm strips of fondant over a small piece of rolled up greaseproof paper and pinch the two ends of each strip together.

Take the third 10cm x 4cm strip and wrap around the ends of the two pinched pieces, to make a bow.

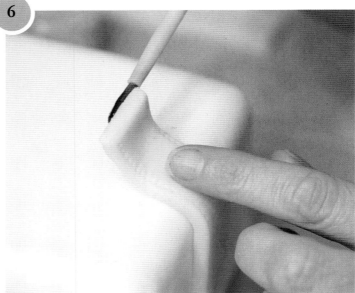

Make two 8 cm x 4 cm trailing bow strips and cut a triangle out of each end to emulate a cut ribbon. Mark along the edge with the wheel tool. Using edible glue stick the 4 strips of 13 cm x 3 cm fondant onto the top and sides of the cake.

**7**

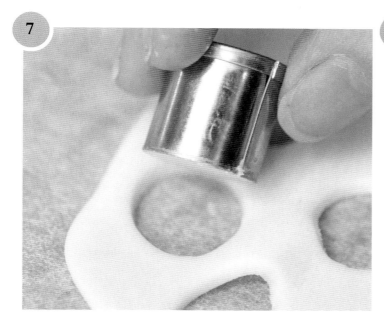

Using a small round cutter cut out 12 small circles and stick these to the sides of the cake.

**8**

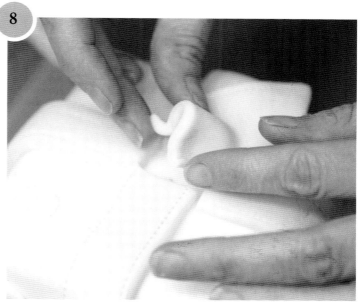

Place the trailing bow strips across two corners of the cake and pinch the ends into the middle to sit underneath the bow.

**9**

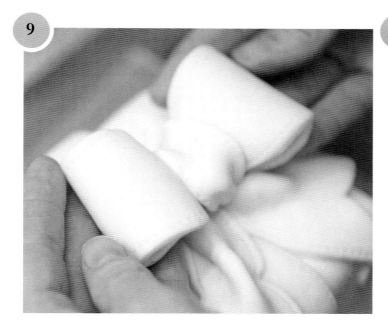

Place the bow on top of the trailing bow strips and remove the greaseproof paper.

**10**

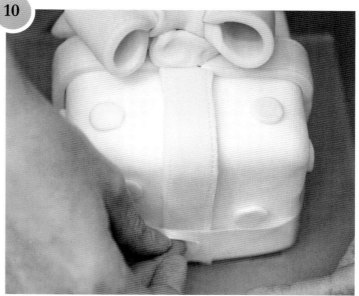

Fix white satin ribbon around the bottom of the cake using double sided adhesive tape.

# White Chocolate Wedding Cake with Fondant Rings and Flowers

## Ingredients

2 large vanilla sponge cakes (see page 14)

500 g / 1 lb 3 oz / 2 ¼ cups royal icing (see page 23)

375 g / 12 oz / 1 cups buttercream

1 large bar white chocolate

250 g / 8 oz / 1 ½ cups of white fondant (see pages 28-29)

green food colouring

yellow food colouring

red food colouring

## SERVES 10-15 | PREP TIME 1 hour

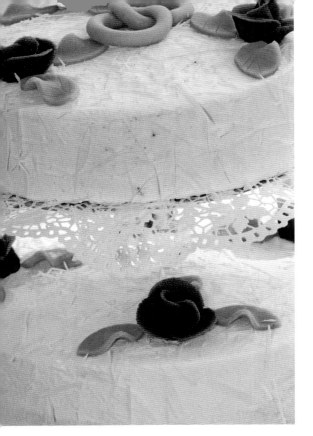

Cover the sponges with a thin layer of buttercream and then spread with the royal icing.

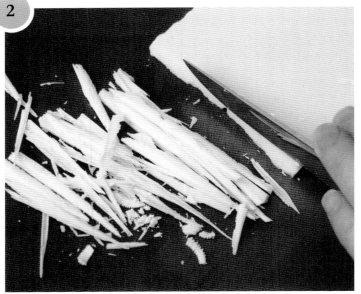

Make shaving of white chocolate by using a sharp knife and pressing down on the edge of the chocolate bar.

**3**

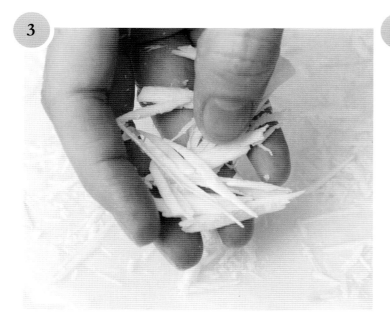

Sprinkle cakes evenly with white chocolate.

**4**

Colour small amounts of fondant with red, yellow and green food colouring. Roll the fondants into 3mm thick sheets. Cut out circles of red fondant and roll them in your fingers to form rose centres. Make as many as you wish. Trim the bottom of the roses, so that they can stand flat against the cake top.

**5**

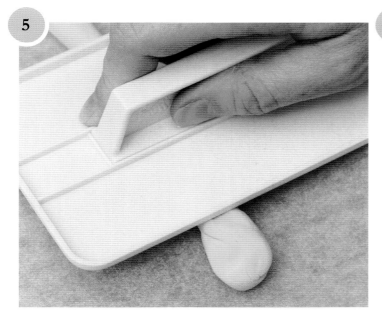

Using a leaf shaped cutter, cut out leaves from the green fondant. Roll the yellow fondant with a cake smoother, cut and form two rings and interlink them.

**6**

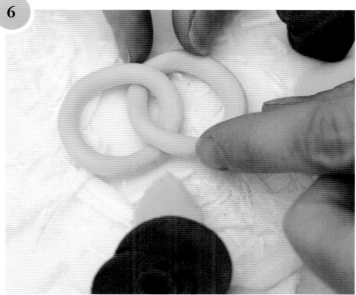

Allow all the fondant to harden. Arrange the roses, rings and leaves on the cakes, place on doilies or cake boards and serve.

# Ivory Rose Cake

## Ingredients

1 heart-shaped vanilla sponge cake
(see page 14)
110 g / 4 oz / ½ cup apricot jam
1 kg / 2 lbs 2 oz / 4 ½ cups ivory fondant
icing (see pages 28-29)

## SERVES 8 | PREP TIME 1 hour

Brush the top and sides of the cake with apricot jam.

Lightly dust the work surface with icing sugar and roll out the icing. Use the rolling pin to help you transport the icing to the cake, then mould it down and over the sides.

152

**3**

Trim away any excess icing and reserve. Use half of the fondant trimmings to make the roses. Flatten small balls of the paste between cellophane and use to make the petals.

**4**

Build the roses up, petal by petal, attaching them with a dab of water.

**5**

Position the roses on top of the cake.

**6**

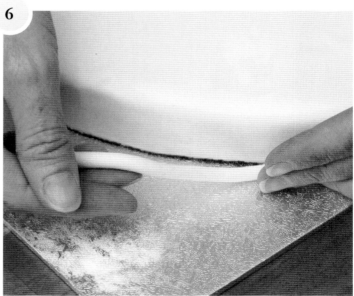

Use a pump action sugarcraft gun to extrude a long strip of fondant icing, then wrap it around the cake where it meets the board.

# Mini Butterfly Cakes

## Ingredients

Three 3" inch vanilla sponge cakes (see page 14)

300 g / 10 oz / 1 ½ cups buttercream

600 g / 1 lb 7 oz / 3 cups coloured fondants (see pages 28-29)

ribbon

silk butterflies

## MAKES 1 | PREP TIME 1 hour

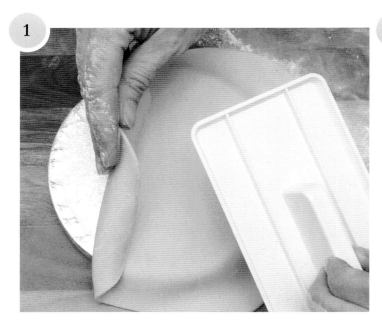

| | |
|---|---|
| **1** Dust a flat surface with icing sugar and roll out the fondant to cover a cake board (approx 3 mm thick). Brush cake board lightly with water to moisten. Using a rolling pin, lift the fondant and lay onto the board. | **2** Using a paddle tool/smoother to smooth over the surface to help the fondant stick and to remove any imperfections. Use a sharp knife to trim the sides and set aside. |

Coat each cake with buttercream using a palette knife.

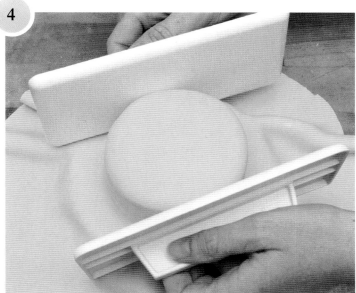

Cover each cake in different coloured fondant and use the smoother to remove and imperfections. Set aside and allow to harden.

Once the fondant is dry, carefully lift the cake onto the cake board and fix a length of ribbon around the cake using double-sided adhesive tape.

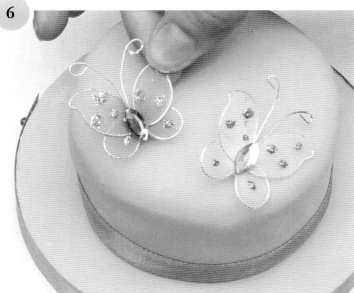

Fix another length of ribbon around the board. Place the silk butterflies on top for decoration.

# Popcorn Bucket Cake

## Ingredients

2 x small 4" round vanilla sponges
(see page 14)

250 g / 9 oz 1 ¼ cups buttercream

500 g / 1 lb 3 oz / 2 ½ cups white fondant
(see pages 28-29)

200 g / 7 oz / 1 cup red fondant
(see pages 28-29)

100 g / 3.5 oz / ½ cup black fondant
(see pages 28-29)

60 g / 2 oz / 3 cups sweet popcorn

## SERVES 6 | PREP TIME 1 hour 30 minutes

Stack the filled sponges and trim to form a bucket shape. Using a tape measure, take measurements of the circumference at the top and at the bottom of the cake and the height.

Cover the cake in buttercream and place it in the refrigerator to set.

**3**

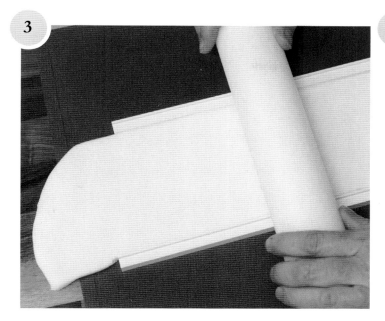

Roll out the white fondant and, using the measurements, cut out a piece long and high enough to wrap around the cake.

**4**

Apply the white fondant around the outside of the cake and smooth using cake smoothers.

**5**

To make the clapper board, cut a square of black fondant and slice a section off one side. Cut out small diamonds out of white fondant and stick them onto the clapper board to form a chevron pattern.

**6**

Cut out the red fondant into strips about 1" wide and to fit the height of the cake. Stick the red stripes onto the sides of the cake, placing the first strip over the seam of the white fondant.

7

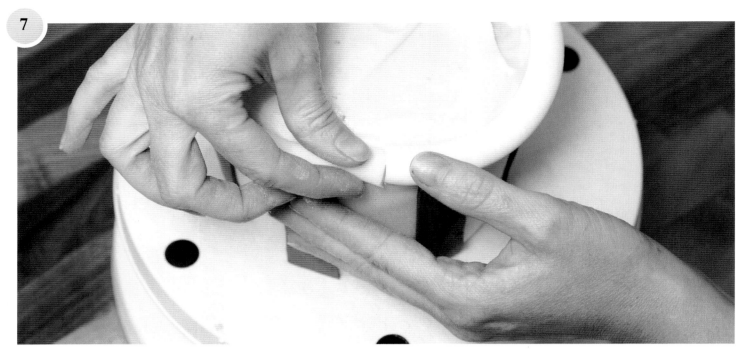

Make a long roll of white fondant to fit around the top of the bucket. Place the rim onto the top of the cake.

8

Arrange the popcorn on top to cover the cake. Stand the clapper board on the side.

# Gingerbread House

## Ingredients

1 square vanilla sponge cake (see page 14)

250 g / 8 oz / 1 cup buttercream

375 g / 13 oz / 2 ¼ cups plain flour

175 g / 6 oz / ½ cup black treacle

½ tsp baking powder

1 tsp ground ginger

1 tsp ground cinnamon

112 g / 4 oz / ½ cup butter

pinch of salt

58 g / 2½ oz / ⅓ cup light soft brown sugar

### To Decorate

150 g / 5 oz / ¾ cup Royal Icing
(see page 23)

150 g / 5 oz / ¾ cup white chocolate buttons

selection of candy (jelly & boiled sweets)

## SERVES 6 | PREP TIME 2 hours

Preheat the oven to 200ºC / 180º fan / 400F / gas 6. In a saucepan, gently heat the butter, sugar, salt and treacle, until the butter has melted.

Sift the flour, baking powder, ginger, cinnamon and in a mixing bowl and pour in the butter mix. Combine well using a dough hook or in a food processor.

Once the dough has come together, wrap it in cling film and rest in the refrigerator for 30 minutes.

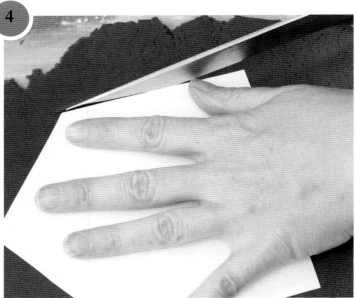

Roll out the dough and cut out pieces using the templates as guides and place on a lined baking sheet. Use shaped cutters to cut out the remaining dough.

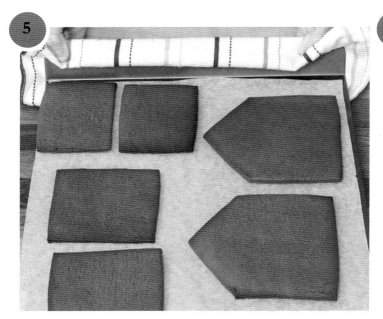

Bake for 15 minutes. Allow to cool slightly on the tray before transferring to a wire rack.

To construct the house, cover a square sponge in buttercream and using royal icing as glue for the edges, stick the side pieces to the cake and allow to set.

7

Using more Royal icing as glue, stick the roof pieces together and glue onto the house and allow to set. Pipe royal icing on the corners and the edges of the roof to hide the seams.

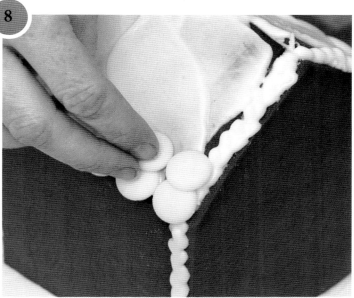

8

Melt 25 g / 1 oz / ¼ cup of the white chocolate and gently smooth it on to the roof. Cover the roof in chocolate buttons, starting at the bottom of the roof and moving towards the apex, to resemble tiles.

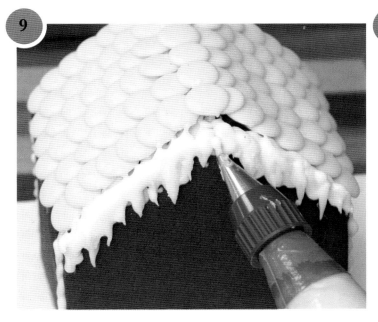

9

Pipe royal icing peaks onto the roof edges to provide a frosted appearance.

10

Pipe out a door and decorate the house and a cake board to make a festive winter theme.

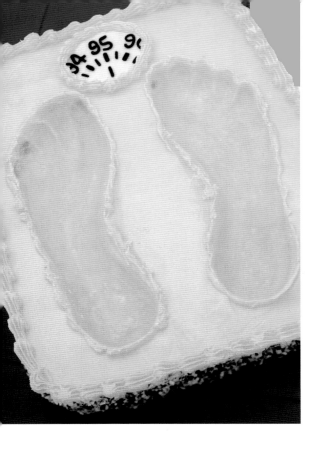

# Scales Cake

## Ingredients

1 large rectangle vanilla sponge (see page 14)

400 g / 14 oz / 2 cups buttercream

20 g / 1 oz / ⅛ cup royal icing (see page 23)

20 g / 1 oz / ⅛ cup of white fondant icing
(see page 28-29)

black food colouring

yellow food colouring

green and yellow candy sprinkles

# SERVES 6 | PREP TIME 1 hour 15 minutes

Colour the buttercream with yellow food colouring. Trim the cake and coat the sides with buttercream. Sprinkle the yellow and green sprinkles on some greaseproof paper. Carefully roll the cake sides in the sprinkles.

Spread yellow buttercream thickly across the top of the cake. Keep some back for piping.

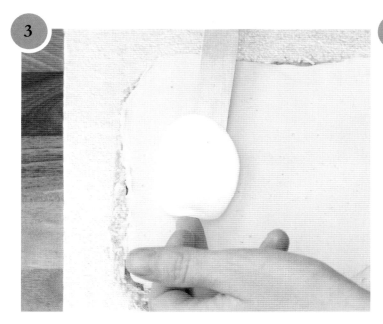

Roll the white fondant into an oval disc and place onto the cake.

Using black food colouring, colour the royal icing and pipe the scale dial onto the oval disc.

Using a medium star nozzle pipe scallops around the edges of the cake.

Using the back of a spoon, indent the buttercream on the top of the cake into footprint shapes.

# Shoe Cupcakes

## Ingredients

12 cupcakes (see page 17)

250 g / 9 oz / 1 cup butter

350 g / 12 oz / 2 ¾ cups icing sugar, sieved

pink food colouring

100 g / 4 oz / ½ cup white fondant (see pages 28-29)

edible sparkles

coloured dragees

50g / 2oz / ¼ cup royal icing (see page 23)

glimmer sugar

## SERVES 12 | PREP TIME 1 hour 15 minutes

Beat the icing sugar and butter and a few drops of pink food colouring together in a bowl until light and fluffy.

Transfer the buttercream in to a piping bag with a large star nozzle. Pipe a swirl of the buttercream onto the cupcakes, starting at the outside and work into the centre.

**3**

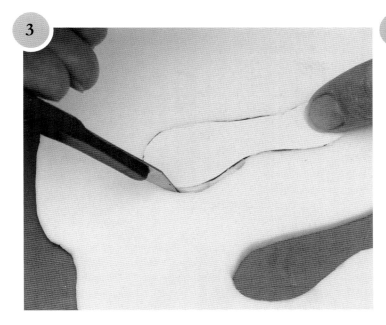

On rolled white fondant, carefully cut out 24 shoe soles using a template and 24 small lengths of fondant for the heels.

**4**

Place the soles on a staggered surface in order to form a raised shoe. Using royal icing form the front of the shoe. Then, carefully pipe a thin line around the sides and back of the sole to build up the shoe.

**5**

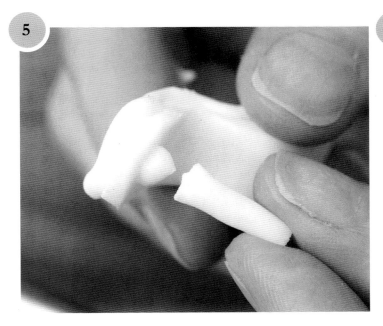

Decorate the front of the shoe with edible sparkles and dragees and allow the soles and the heels to set. Then, glue the heels to the underside of the soles using royal icing.

**6**

Decorate the cupcakes with the shoes, sparkles, glimmer sugar and dragees.

# Spider Cake

## Ingredients

20 cm / 8" chocolate sponge
(see page 15)
50 g / 1 ¾ oz / ¼ cup apricot jam
50 g / 1 ¾ oz / ¼ cup royal icing
(see page 23)
1 chocolate covered tea cake
chocolate vermicelli
10 g / ⅓ oz / 1 tsp white fondant
(see pages 28-29)
2 orange hard shelled chocolate candy

1 packet glace cherries
40 g / 1 ½ oz / ¼ cup brown fondant
(see pages 28-29)
8 small chocolate balls

### For the sauce

240 g / 8 ½ oz / 2 cups dark chocolate
70 ml water
90 g / 3 oz / ½ cup sugar

## SERVES 4-6 | PREP TIME 45 minutes

Trim the sides and top of a chocolate sponge.

Brush the cake with apricot jam.

**3**

Pour over the icing and allow to drip down the sides of the cake.

**4**

Using a piping bag, pipe lines of white icing out from the centre of the cake to the edges.

**5**

Starting from the centre, pipe a spiral. As you move outwards towards the edges of the cake, scallop the icing to make a web.

**6**

Brush the tea cake with some apricot jam and sprinkle over the chocolate vermicelli.

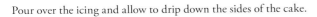

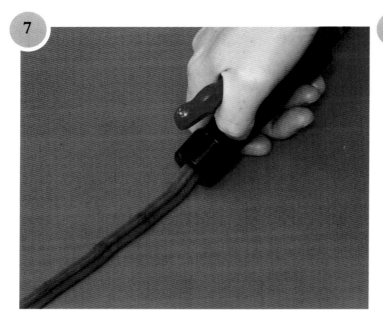

Using a sugar paste gun, create a long strip and cut into 8 pieces to form the legs of the spider.

Make teeth out of fondant and then stick onto the spider using royal icing.

Assemble the cake by sticking the legs onto the teacake using melted chocolate.

Dress the cake with the cherries and chocolate balls.

# Chocolate Mask Cake

## Ingredients

15 cm / 6" round chocolate sponge
(see page 15)
250 g / 9 oz / 1 ½ cups dark chocolate, for
the mask

### For the sauce

250 g / 9 oz / 1 ½ cups good quality dark
chocolate
70 ml / 2.4 fl. oz / ⅓ cup
90 g / 3 oz / ½ cup sugar

# SERVES 8 | PREP TIME 1 hour

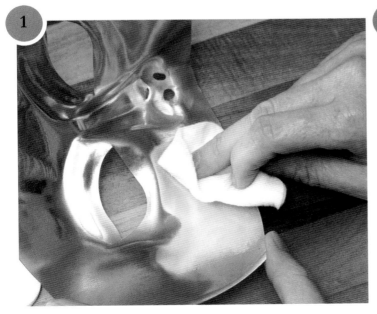

Polish the inside of the mask using dry cotton wool.

Melt the chocolate over a bain-marie.

**3**

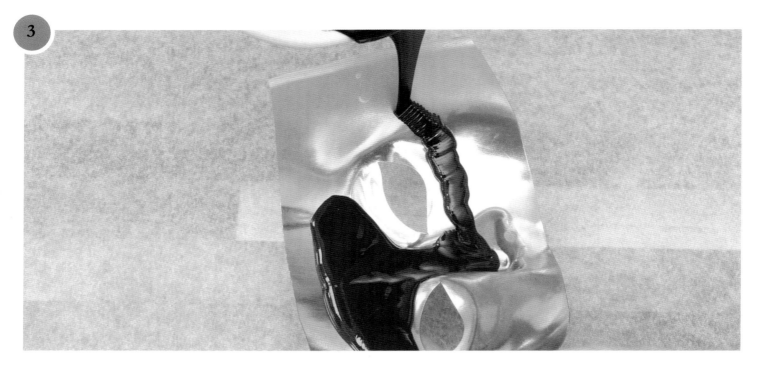

Pour the chocolate into the mask mould and coat the surface evenly.

**4**

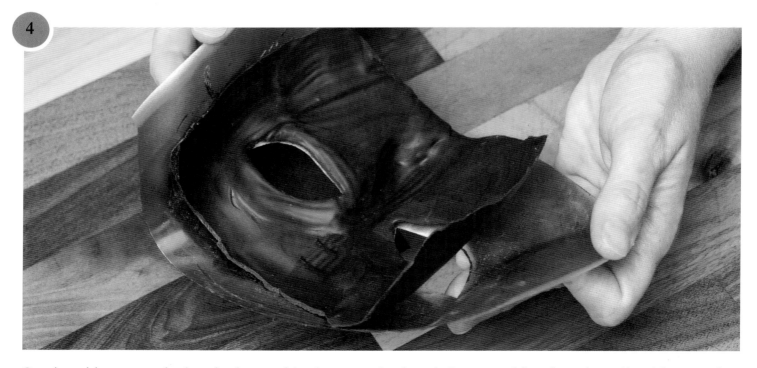

Once the mask has set pour or brush another thin coat of chocolate to strengthen the mask. Once set, carefully peel away the mould. Boil the water and sugar in a saucepan, then allow to cool.

170

**5**

Melt the chocolate in a heatproof bowl over a pan of simmering water. Remove from the heat. Add the syrup, a spoonful at a time, to the chocolate and whisk to combine, then allow to cool.

**6**

Pour the cooled sauce over the cake.

**7**

Carefully position the mask onto the cake and light sparklers at the time of serving.

# Pink Princess Cake

## Ingredients

1 x 20 cm / 8"round chocolate sponge cake
(see page 15)

1 kg / 2 lbs 2 oz / 4 ½ cups pink fondant
icing (see pages 28-29)

55 g / 2 oz / ¼ cup brown fondant icing
(see pages 28-29)

55 g / 2 oz / ¼ cup purple fondant icing
(see pages 28-29)

55 g / 2 oz / ¼ cup blue fondant icing
(see pages 28-29)

55 g / 2 oz / ¼ cup royal icing
(see pages 28-29)

coloured sugar pearls

pink ribbon

## SERVES 8 | PREP TIME 3 hours

Cover the cake with the pink fondant icing, using a cake smoother to get a smooth, professional finish. Trim away any excess icing. Make the princess's face and arms with the pink icing trimmings.

Use a pump action sugarcraft gun to extrude the brown icing for the hair.

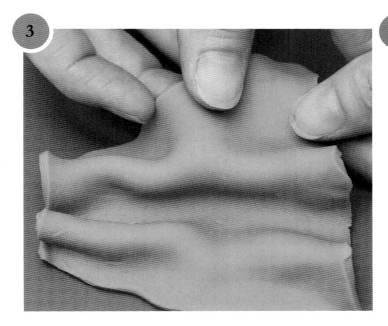

Make the dress from the purple icing by rolling it out thinly and gathering it slightly on top of the cake.

Cut out flower shapes from the blue and purple icing and stick them to the cake with a dab of water.

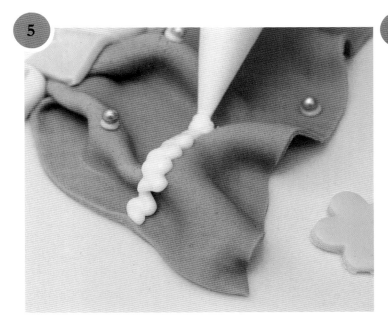

Pipe the final details onto the princess with royal icing and attach the sugar pearls.

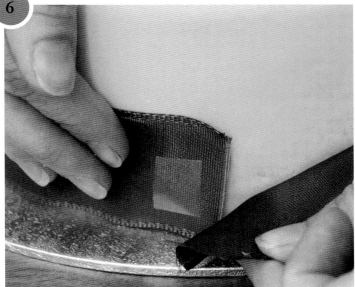

Wrap the ribbon around the cake and fix in place with a small square of double-sided tape.

# Raspberry Mousse Cake

## Ingredients

55 g / 2 oz / ¼ cup light pink fondant icing (see pages 28-29)

55 g / 2 oz / ¼ cup dark pink fondant icing (see pages 28-29)

400 g / 14 oz / 2 ½ cups raspberries

4 tbsp caster sugar

½ oz powdered gelatine

200 ml / 6 ½ fl. oz / ¾ cup double cream, whipped

1 heart-shaped sponge cake, split into 3
horizontally (see page 34)

## SERVES 8 | PREP TIME 1 hour

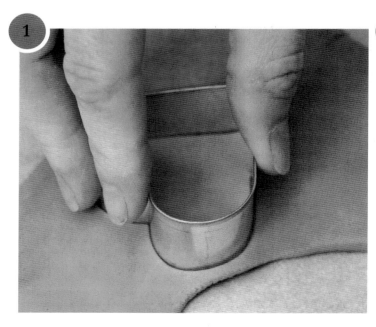

Roll out the light and dark pink fondant icing and cut out a heart shape
from each.

Dissolve the gelatine in some warm water. Blend ¾ of the raspberries to a
puree and strain into a saucepan. Heat the raspberry puree with the caster
sugar until it dissolves.

Pour the raspberry puree and sugar mixture into a bowl and stir in half of the gelatine until it dissolves.

Put 1 of the cakes back into its tin and pour half of the raspberry puree mixture on top. Chill until set. Fold the other half of the raspberry mixture into the whipped cream with the rest of the gelatine to form the mousse.

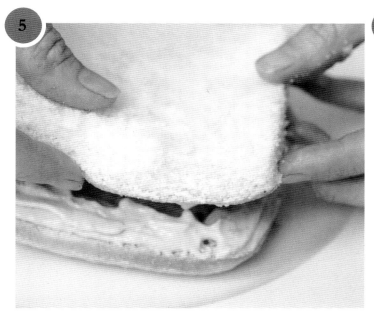

Spoon 1/3 of the mousse onto the base cake. Top with the middle cake and spread with another third of the mousse.

Top with the jelly cake layer and arrange 2 fondants hearts on top. Spoon the remaining mousse into a piping bag and pipe around the edge of the cake. Top with the raspberries and allow to chill and set for 2 hours.

# Handbag Cake

## Ingredients

20 cm / 8" large square vanilla sponge cake (see page 14)

400 g / 1 lb / 1 ¾ cups buttercream

1 large packet of strawberry laces

jelly sweets / candy

1 meter strawberry strip liquorice candy

yellow hard shelled chocolate sweets / candy

yellow food colouring

pink food colouring

50 g / 1 ¾ oz / ½ cup Royal icing (see page 23)

# SERVES 6-8 | PREP TIME 45 minutes

Take the sponge cake and slice in half.

Turn one slice over and cover with jam and buttercream.

176

**3**

Place the cake slices together back to back with the buttercream and jam sandwiched together.

**4**

Trim the cakes so that they resemble the handbag shape.

**5**

Colour the buttercream with a little pink food colouring. Coat the cake in a thick layer of pink buttercream.

**6**

Cut the strips of strawberry strip liquorice candy to the width of the handbag and apply in rows to make the bag flap. Cut triangles of the strawberry strip liquorice candy and stick to the corners of the handbag.

**7**

Using a flower shaped cutter cut flowers out of the remaining strawberry strip liquorice candy and stick to the cake.

**8**

Make the bag handle from strawberry laces wrapped around an arched piece of paper covered confectioners wire. Place on top of the cake.

**9**

Colour the Royal icing with a little yellow food colouring and pipe stitches around the bag flap.

**10**

Stick yellow hard shelled chocolate sweets / candy to the middle of the flowers with piped icing. Scatter the jelly candy around the base of the cake.

# Chocolate Castle Cake

## Ingredients

1 x 26 cm/ 10" square chocolate sponge cake
(see page 15)

half quantity of chocolate sponge cake
mixture (see page 15)

4 ice cream cones

400 g / 14 oz milk chocolate, melted

chocolate biscuit fingers

small sweets

## SERVES 10 | PREP TIME 1 hour 30 minutes

Preheat the oven to 190⁰C (170⁰ fan) / 375F / gas 5. Prepare and measure all of the ingredients.

Spread the sponge cake mixture out in a baking tin to 1 cm / ½" thick and bake for 10 minutes.

Test with a wooden toothpick, if it comes out clean, the cake is done. Transfer the cake to a wire rack and leave to cool completely. Cut out 4 circles of cake using a pastry cutter, they should be the same circumference as the ice cream cones.

Use the cake circles to steady the ice cream cones while you brush them with melted chocolate. Leave in a cool place for the chocolate to set.

Pour the rest of the chocolate over the cake and spread it out with a pallet knife.

Transfer the cake circles to the top of the cake.

Top the cake circles with the chocolate ice cream cones.

Cut the chocolate fingers into small pieces and set them round the outside edge of the cake.

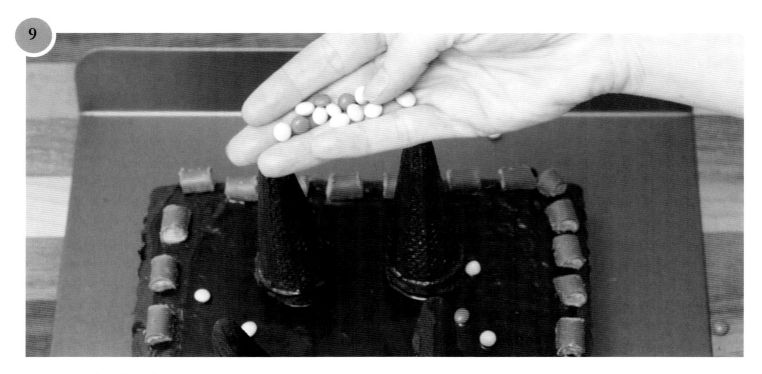

Sprinkle the cake with small sweets.

# Violin Cake

## Ingredients

1 litre / 1 ¾ pints / 4 cups chocolate ice-cream

2 brandy snaps

50 g / 1 ¾ oz / ¼ cup chocolate fondant (see pages 28-29)

20 g / ¾ oz red fondant (see pages 28-29)

20 g / ¾ oz green fondant (see pages 28-29)

20 g / ¾ oz chocolate ganache (see page 22)

20 g / ¾ oz royal icing (see page 23)

## SERVES 4-6 | PREP TIME 1 hour

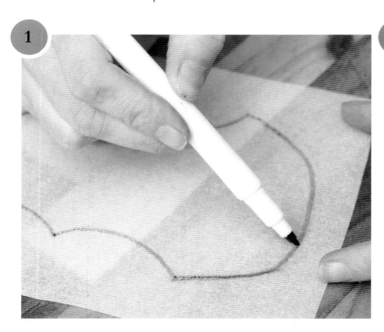

On parchment paper draw a violin shape using an edible icing pen. Cut a block of ice cream into the shape of a violin and place in the freezer.

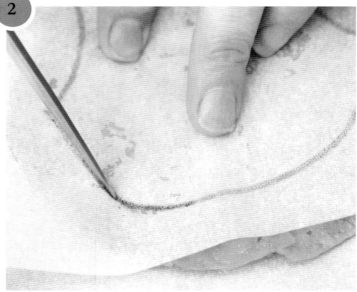

Heat the brandy snaps in the oven to uncurl. Remove from the oven and whilst they are still warm cut out a violin shape using the parchment template.

**3**

Roll and cut out a piece of chocolate fondant into the shape of the chin rest and neck of the violin.

**4**

Remove the ice cream violin from the freezer and arrange the chocolate fondant shapes and brandy snap shape on top.

**5**

Stamp out a leaf from the green fondant icing and create a rose from the red fondant icing. Fill a piping bag with the royal icing.

**6**

Pipe swirls onto the top of the neck to form the scroll and lines to represent the strings.

# Ice Cream Cake

## Ingredients

500 ml / 17 fl. oz / 1 pint strawberry ice cream

2 tbsp soured cream

300 ml / 10 ½ fl. oz / 1 ¼ cups raspberry ice cream

300 ml / 10 ½ fl. oz / 1 ¼ cups pistachio ice cream

300 ml / 10 ½ fl. oz / 1 ¼ cups mango ice cream

3 brandy snaps

red currants

## SERVES 4 | PREP TIME 1 hour

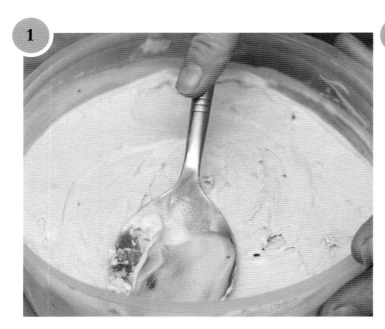

Preheat the oven to 180°C (160° fan) / 350F / gas 4. Press the strawberry ice cream into the bottom of a plastic cake mould and freeze until firm.

Use an ice cream scoop to shape balls from the other ice creams and make a rose pattern in the surface with a knife.

**3**

Spread the ice cream balls out on a baking tray and freeze until firm. Spread the brandy snaps out on a baking tray and put them in the oven for 2 – 3 minutes or until they become pliable.

**4**

Make a horn shape out of scrunched up tin foil. When the brandy snaps come out of the oven, mould them around the foil horn and leave to cool and set.

**5**

Take the ice cream cake out of the freezer and spread the top with soured cream. Place back into the freezer to set.

**6**

Lay the brandy snap horn on its side and arrange the frozen ice cream balls to the side. Decorate with sprigs of fresh red currants.

# Chocolate Hedgehog Cake

## Ingredients

1 vanilla sponge cooked in an 6" basin (see page 14)

1 packet of plain chocolate sticks

1 packet of white chocolate sticks

50 g / 1 ⅔ oz / ¼ cup apricot jam

240 g / 8 ½ oz / 2 cups plain chocolate, melted

70 ml / 2 ½ fl. oz / ⅓ cup water and 100g / 3 ½ oz / ½ cup sugar made into syrup

1 small pack of chocolate vermicelli decorations

1 small pack of multi-coloured sprinkles

2 marshmallows

1 piece of red liquorice, filled with fondant sliced into discs

1 yellow liquorice comfort

1 piece of pink liquorice bobble candy boiled candy to scatter

# SERVES 4-6 | PREP TIME 45 minutes

Coat the sponge cake with the jam.

Make up the chocolate icing by mixing the sugar syrup with the melted chocolate until you have a smooth thick consistency.

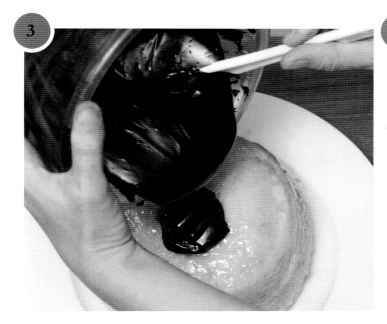

Pour over the icing and smooth around the cake to coat evenly.

When it begins to set sprinkle with chocolate vermicelli. Stick the different chocolate sticks into the cake to make the hedgehog spines.

Place the yellow liquorice onto the cake for the mouth and the pink liquorice bobble candy for the nose.

Stick the red liquorice filled slices to the marshmallows with a little water, and then stick to the cake for the eyes. Sprinkle the multi-coloured sprinkles around the cake bottom and scatter the boiled candy.

# Football Cake

## Ingredients

1 large square or rectangle vanilla sponge
(see page 14)

1kg green fondant (see pages 28-29)

1 football pitch fondant transfer

200 g / 7 oz / 1 cup flesh coloured fondant
(see pages 28-29)

50 g / 1 ¾ oz / ¼ cup blue fondant
(see pages 28-29)

50 g / 1 ¾ oz / ¼ cup red fondant
(see pages 28-29)

100 g / 3 ½ oz / ½ cup black fondant
(see pages 28-29)

10 g / ⅓ oz / 1 tbsp white fondant
(see pages 28-29)

10 g / ⅓ oz / 1 tbsp yellow fondant
(see pages 28-29)

1 black edible food pen

2 plastic football goals

## SERVES 8 | PREP TIME 2 hours

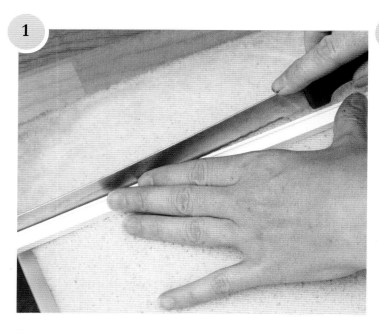

Trim a sponge to the same size as the fondant transfer. Fill the sponge with buttercream and jam. Coat the sponge is buttercream and place in the refrigerator to set.

Cover the cake using green fondant and allow to harden.

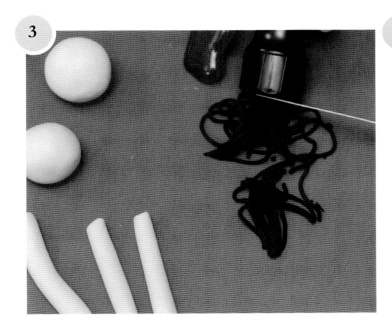

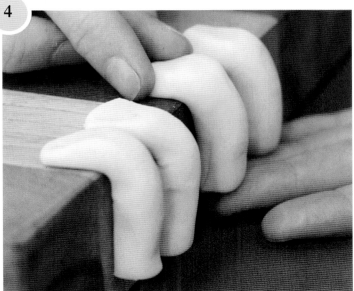

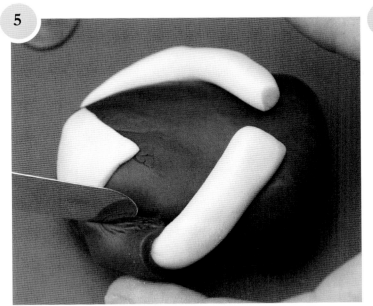

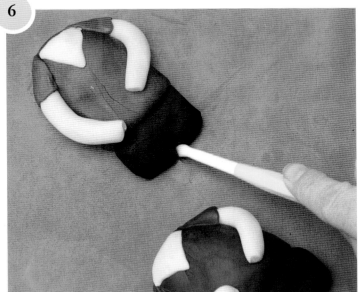

**7**

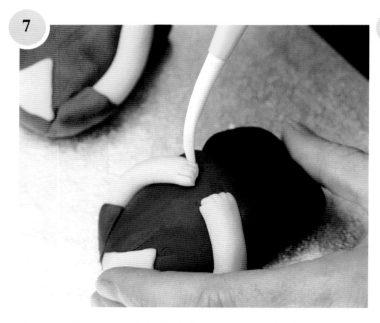

Now assemble the parts of the footballers by gluing the heads onto the shirts. Stick the top half of the footballers onto the shorts and then stick on the legs.

**8**

Create football boots by piping thin white lines of royal icing onto small balls of black fondant. Stick these to the legs using edible glue.

**9**

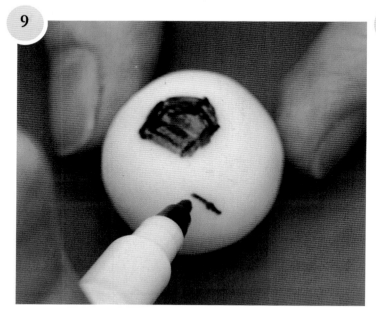

For the whistle, roll a ball of white fondant and pinch one side to make the mouthpiece. Paint with edible silver dust. Roll a football out of white fondant. Draw on black hexagons using an edible pen.

**10**

Carefully position the fondant transfer onto the cake and set aside. Arrange the players, goals, football, referee cards and whistle onto the cake.

# Index